MW00998060

Claudia Roden's
Mediterranean

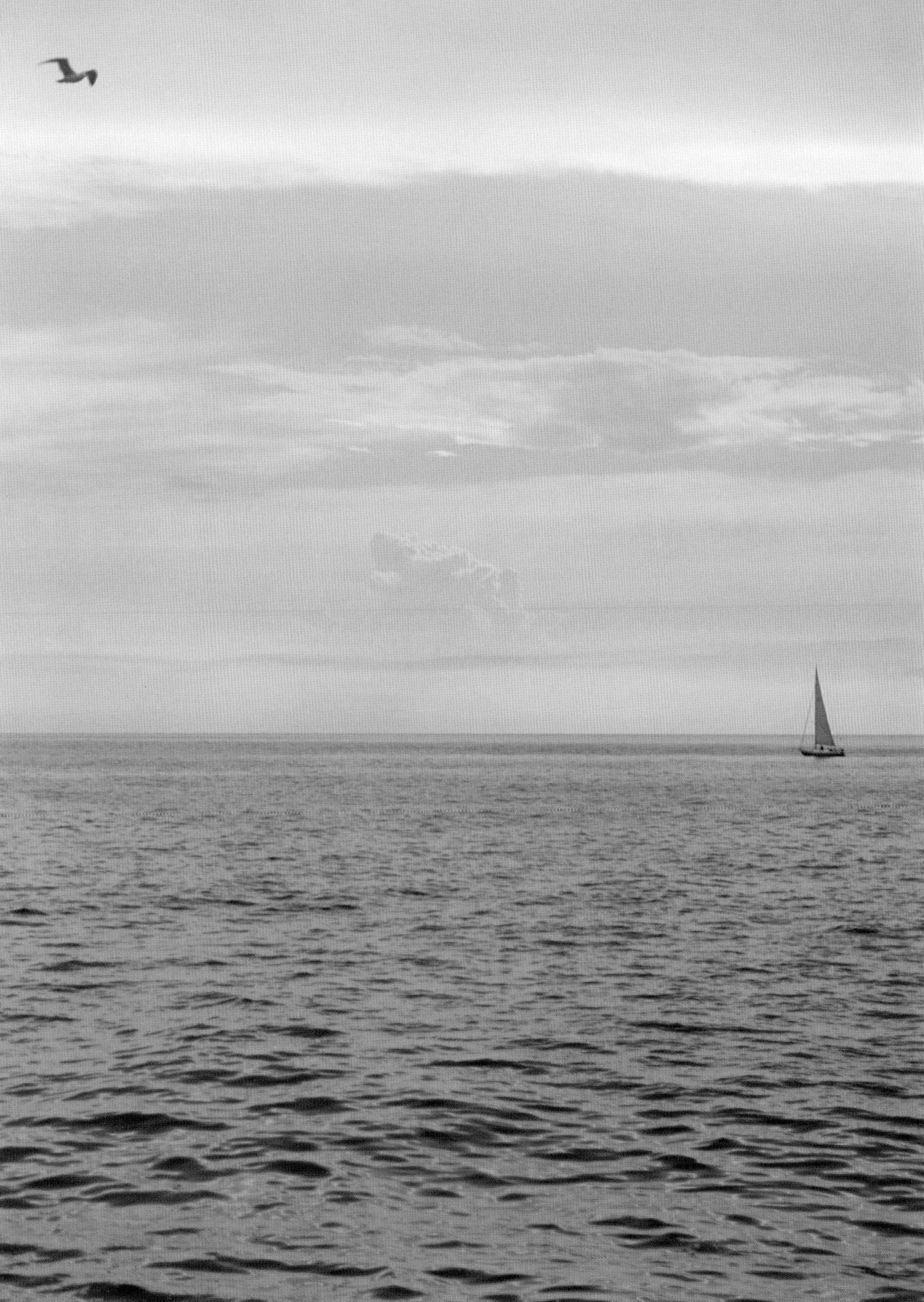

Claudia Roden's Mediterranean

TREASURED RECIPES FROM A LIFETIME OF TRAVEL

TEN SPEED PRESS
California | New York

For my children, Simon, Nadia, and Anna; my grandchildren, Cesar, Peter, Sarah, Ruby, Nelly, and Lily. And for Clive and Ros; my brother Ellis and sister-in-law Gill.

"Cooking is the landscape in a saucepan."
—Josep Pla

CONTENTS

INTRODUCTION

An adventure that never ended

When my three children left home all at the same time thirty-five years ago, I decided to leave, too, and travel around the Mediterranean. I went alone, à l'aventure – without plans or arrangements.

A childhood memory lived inside me of the exhilarating moment we arrived in Alexandria by the desert road from our home in Cairo and suddenly saw the sea. To me, Alexandria was a different world, with other trees and flowers and new smells and villas painted yellow and pink. Compared to the serious and restrained Cairo, it was a city of freedom and pleasure. You felt the exuberant lighthearted mood in the cafés along the seafront. Italian, Greek, and French were spoken in the street. The city was part of another world, one to which Marseille and Barcelona, Genoa, Athens and Algiers, Beirut and Tangier also belonged. That world had a culture all of its own, so powerful that the whole country was influenced as though the sea was its center of gravity.

I wanted to find that spirit again.

Back in the 1980s, a woman traveling alone was strange and suspect, but researching food gave me a mission and a reason to be there. It allowed me to make contacts, to ask for help, and to spend time in restaurant kitchens. It allowed me to accost people and introduce myself on trains, in cafés, or in the sitting rooms of pensions, or small hotels. I would start a conversation with "I'm an English food writer researching your cuisine. Can you tell me what your favorite dishes are?" They didn't always buy the "English," but were always happy to talk about their food. My interest was in home cooking and regional food. I was invited into homes where people still cooked as their parents and grandparents did. Part of the pleasure of researching food was meeting people, sharing a moment of their lives, and discovering their worlds. There is a special conviviality and intimacy in the kitchen that you don't quite get in the living room.

The Mediterranean has remained the focus of my work. This book is based on remembered dishes that I have encountered over decades. Working on it has kept me happy, thinking of people and places, magic moments, and glorious food. It might be cold and gray and raining outside, but in my kitchen and at my desk in London I am smiling under an azure sky. The smell of garlic sizzling with crushed coriander seeds takes me back to the Egypt of my childhood. The aroma of saffron and orange zest mingled with aniseed and garlic triggers memories of the French Riviera. I still cook the dishes in this collection for family and friends. They capture so well the special charm and spirit of a world that enthralls me.

A world of its own

The countries around the Mediterranean Sea are very different: Eastern and Western, Christian and Muslim, with forests, deserts, mountains, bays, and islands. But they also have a lot in common. A shared climate, with hot dry summers, mild winters, and balmy air, encourages an easygoing outdoor life, alfresco eating, street foods, and markets. An incestuous history, with the same empires, occupiers, settlers, and movements of populations, and intense sea traffic and trading activities between port cities, have created a food culture that is immensely varied, unique, and different from anywhere else in the world. Hospitality is an important part of the culture, and meals are a time of interaction. The custom of serving an assortment of little dishes with drinks is part of the relaxed way of life where you are supposed to enjoy the moment and the company in an unhurried way.

Every country has its own cuisine and unique dishes, and the cooking differs between town and rural area and from one town or village to another, but I also had a feeling of déjà vu in kitchens from one end of the sea to the other. I saw the same produce in the markets – the same vegetables, pulses, and grains, the same fruits and nuts, great piles of olives, the same preserved vegetables. The meat is lamb, and also goat, hare, and rabbit, with pork in Christian countries. There is not enough humidity nor the right terrain for pastures and cattle raising so beef is not common, but chickens are plentiful and there are also ducks and migrating quails.

I saw the same utensils – clay pots that can go on top of the fire, mortars and pestles, skewers, the same wood-burning outdoor ovens. And I found similar dishes. The brandade of salt cod in Provence is the same as the baccalà of Venice or the bacalao of Catalonia. Chicken is cooked with grapes in Spain as it is in Tuscany. The octopus stews of Greece are like those of Provence. There are eggplant purées and fava bean purées everywhere, and you also find vegetable omelets and stuffed vegetables, rice puddings and almond pastries, sauces thickened with bread, ground almonds, pine nuts, or walnuts. Tomato sauce is the signature tune of the entire Mediterranean, olives and garlic are its symbols.

Spuntineria
Enoteca
Bar
illy
Mercoledì
chiuso

Despite the similarities, there are distinct differences. Where the French use cognac, Sicilians use Marsala, and Spaniards sherry. Where Italians use mozzarella, Parmesan, pecorino, or ricotta; the French use goat cheese or Gruyère; and the Greeks, Turks, Lebanese, and Egyptians use feta or halloumi. Where an Egyptian or Syrian would use ground almonds or pine nuts in a sauce, a Turk uses walnuts. Crème fraîche is used in France where yogurt and buffalo-milk cream are used in the eastern Mediterranean. In the northern Mediterranean, the flavors are of herbs that grow wild; in the eastern and southern Mediterranean, they are of spices, flower waters, and molasses. In Turkey they flavor their meats with cinnamon and allspice, in Morocco they use cumin, saffron, cinnamon, and ginger. While a fish soup in the French Midi includes orange zest and saffron, in Tunisia it will have cumin, paprika, cayenne, and cilantro leaves. It's as if the common language of the Mediterranean is spoken in myriad dialects.

Memories of life in old rural worlds live on in the cooking, like ghosts hovering in saucepans

Many Mediterranean dishes are simple and frugal, reflecting the rural lives of people before they began leaving the land for cities, before agriculture was industrialized and tourism became the main industry, before seasonal immigrant workers did the harvesting. The old peasantry could rarely afford meat. In some countries, it was eaten only on festive occasions. In Christian countries, it was forbidden by the church on Fridays and during Lent. That is why grains, pulses, vegetables, fruit, and nuts have a very important place in so many of these dishes.

An important rural tradition was the preservation of food, a means of survival when seasons alternated dramatically between short periods of great abundance and long ones of scarcity. Fruits and vegetables were laid out on trays in the fields to dry in the sun, preserved in brine or oil, or made into jams or pickles. Tomatoes were reduced to paste. Olives were cured and pickled or crushed for their oil. Grains, pulses, and nuts were dried on rooftops. Meats were cooked slowly and preserved in their fat or turned into pâtés or terrines. Pork was cured and dried as ham, or made into salami. In Turkey, the Balkans, and the Levant, yogurt was drained to make a soft cheese that was rolled into balls and preserved in olive oil. The juice of sour pomegranates was boiled down to syrupy molasses. Distilled rose and orange blossom waters were produced by boiling petals in alembics. Nowadays, all these things are mass-produced and we can find them as delicacies in our supermarkets.

Sophisticated Mediterranean dishes are a legacy of a glittering past

In addition to these rural traditions, there are refinements that hark back to the powerful empires that have come and gone around the Mediterranean. The Romans spread the classical triad of bread, wine, and olive oil across the entire region. The Arabs introduced irrigation techniques, new crops, and horticultural and cooking practices and brought spices and aromatics from the East. The Ummayad Caliphate, from its capital, Damascus, extended its empire through North Africa all the way to Spain. It was succeeded by the Abbasid Caliphate, whose capital was Baghdad; the grand styles of ancient Persia were adopted by the Caliphate elite, and their tastes still echo in Spain, Sicily, and North Africa. Among the Arab legacies are sweet-and-sour and savory-and-sweet combinations, meats cooked with fruit, milk puddings, and almond pastries. Whenever you see raisins and pine nuts in a local dish, you know that Arabs were in the region at one point.

Rich, refined dishes, developed in the court kitchens of Constantinople (now Istanbul) when it was the capital of the Ottoman Empire, appeared throughout that empire, which covered much of the eastern Mediterranean and northern Africa for more than five hundred years. Barcelona, once the merchant queen of the Mediterranean, had a strong influence on cooking, as had the Republic of Venice, which once had colonies and trading posts as far afield as Alexandria. And the revelation of the New World at the end of the fifteenth century brought new foods and revolutionized the Mediterranean diet. It's hard to imagine the food of the Mediterranean without tomatoes and peppers.

A book of food for family and friends

Working on this book has allowed me to keep doing what I love: cooking and spending time with friends and family. I invited two or three or four at a time to try dishes over regular little dinners around my kitchen table to find what gave us the most pleasure. I woke up excited, imagining dishes and planning menus. I devised easy meals that I could handle alone. Like everyone today, I did not want to spend hours in the kitchen and wished to enjoy the company of my friends. I wanted to please and hoped to enthrall. Some of the guests at my table were as old as I am, some were my children's and grandchildren's ages. Many were vegetarian, a few were vegan, or gluten- or dairy-intolerant. I took that into consideration when planning my menus and that is reflected in my choice of recipes. I love meat, but am happier now to eat much less. The ingredients I use represent what has long been seen as the healthful "Mediterranean diet": rich in grains, vegetables, fruit, and nuts, with plenty of fish but little meat, and olive oil as the main cooking fat.

Flavors range from very delicate through sharp, sweet-and-sour, and savory-and-sweet to complex and spicy hot. There is almost always garlic and olive oil, often lemon and tomatoes, herbs and spices, sometimes anchovies, olives, and chiles. Spirits and wines are used in the northern and western Mediterranean; aromatics such as orange blossom and rose waters and pomegranate molasses are used in the east and south. Simple dishes are enlivened by sauces – extra-virgin olive oil blended with garlic and an herb; versions of aïoli and nutty creams; yogurt with garlic; lemon; or tahini.

In my previous books, I have featured hundreds of traditional Middle Eastern and Mediterranean dishes that were new in Britain at the time and are now part of our modern English cuisine, with everyone doing their own take. With this book, I wanted to offer something different. A few of the recipes are updated versions of dishes that have appeared before. But the majority are entirely new. Many are French, because I have had a studio in Paris for thirty-two years, and during this time the cooking of the south became the most popular in France. There are classics and little-known traditional specialties. I have felt free to simplify and refine, to intensify flavors and make dishes more beautiful, sometimes to interpret and innovate while still keeping their traditional character.

The aim of this book is to highlight what to me is the best of the Mediterranean and adapt it for the way we like to eat today. It is what I cook when I entertain friends and family. I hope you will get as much pleasure from the dishes as we did and make them your own.

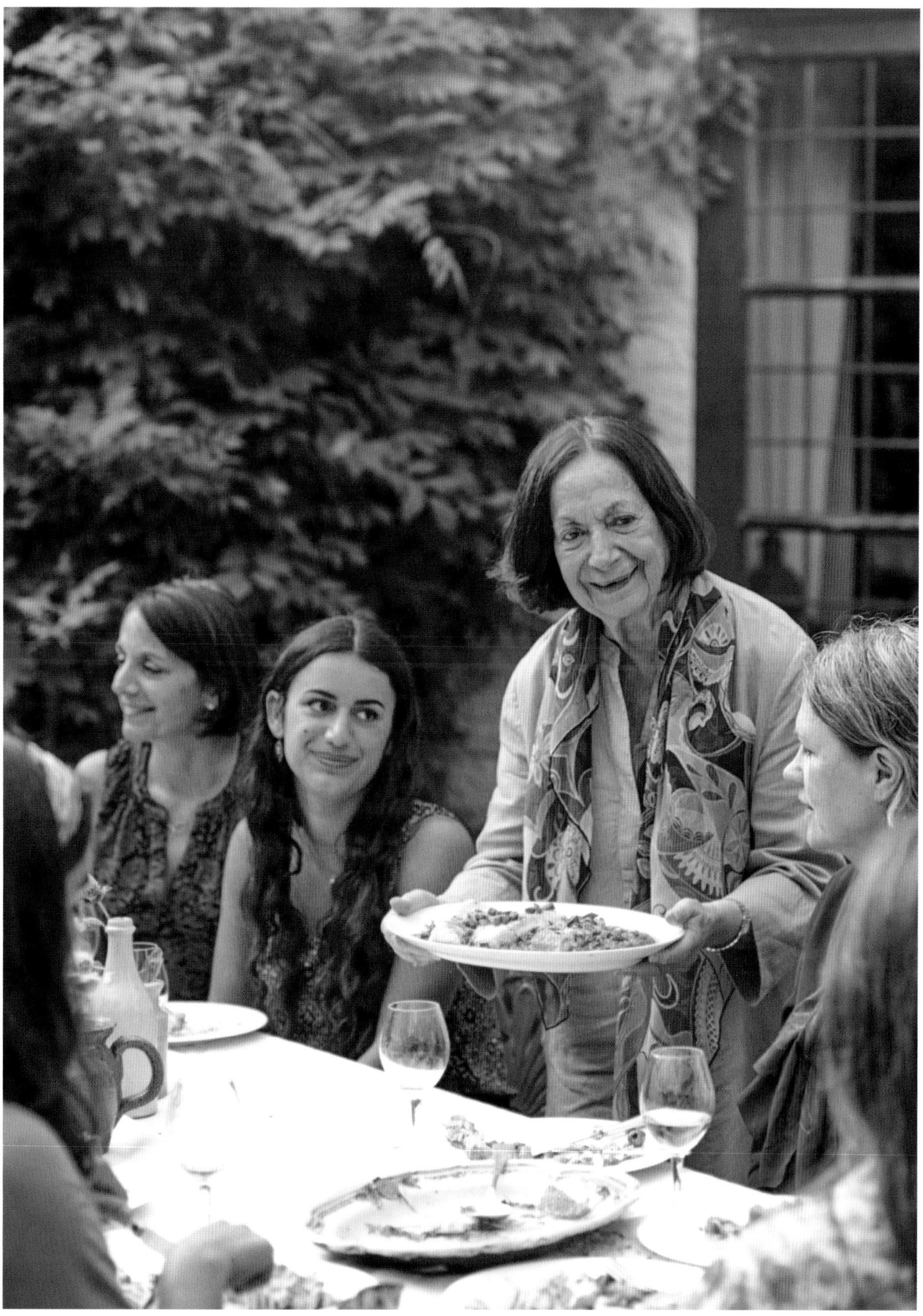

WHERE MY TASTES COME FROM

I was born in 1936. The Egypt that I grew up in was a cosmopolitan world where people spoke many languages, and French was the lingua franca. I lived with my parents, Cesar and Nelly Douek; my brothers, Ellis and Zaki; and our Slovene Italian nanny, Maria Koron, in a quarter of Cairo that was an island, called Zamalek, in the Nile. We were part of two large extended families. Three of my grandparents came to Egypt from Aleppo at the end of the nineteenth century when the Suez Canal was built and Egypt became a mercantile hub. My maternal grandmother was from Istanbul. Her ancestors were banished from Spain in 1492. She spoke a medieval Judeo-Spanish, but had trained as a teacher in Paris and was like a missionary for French culture. When we were small, Maria cooked for us what she knew. Awad, our cook, learned from my mother how to cook the dishes that were passed down in our families: phyllo cigars, kibbeh, tabbouleh, baba ghanouj, konafa, milk puddings, almond cakes – and French food.

In 1951, at fifteen, I was sent to boarding school in Paris, because Zaki had to be there after an operation and Ellis was there studying medicine. On weekends, I slept on sofas at relatives' and day students' homes, and at the hotel Monsieur le Prince in the Latin Quarter where Ellis had a room. I hung around with friends and got to know céleri rémoulade, poule au pot, hachis parmentier, and chaussons aux pommes.

I came to London to study art at Saint Martin's in 1954. Ellis had also moved to medical school in London, and Zaki joined us and attended the French Lycée. We had a flat and I cooked for them and for our student friends. I spent hours rolling grape leaves and making stuffed vegetables. The only place where I could buy what I needed for our kind of food – bulgur, chickpeas, tahini, pomegranate molasses, rose water – was at Mrs. Haral's in Camden Town. In the workshop of Olympia, in Kentish Town, I could buy pita and kadaifi and watch artisans make phyllo by hand.

I started collecting recipes in 1956, when the Jews were forced to leave Egypt after the Suez War, and my parents joined us. For many years, we were inundated with refugees from Egypt passing through, looking for a country to settle in. People exchanged recipes. We thought we would never see each other again, so recipes were something to remember one another by. There had been no cookbooks in Egypt. What I collected was a mixed bag because the Jewish community of Egypt was a mosaic of families from all over the old Ottoman world and from around the Mediterranean.

When I married and had children, I was always trying the recipes to make them work because the instructions were not precise. "You'll know that there is enough flour when the dough feels like your earlobe"; "the smell will tell you when it's ready." I went on and on collecting. I was smitten. I hung around places such as carpet warehouses and embassies, where I could meet people from the Middle East and ask for recipes. When I asked a librarian at the British Library to help me find books on Arab food, he came up with a list of translations of medieval culinary manuals. There was nothing contemporary. That is when I became interested in the history and origins of dishes and the cultures behind them.

When I decided to turn the recipes into a book and told people, they said "Why don't you paint?" Writing about food was not the hot subject it is now. And when I said I was researching Middle Eastern dishes, they said "is it sheeps' eyes and testicles?" My *New Book of Middle Eastern Food* and the books that followed became primary

sources for chefs and food writers discovering Middle Eastern and Mediterranean cuisines.

Writing about food was how I supported the family when my marriage split up and I became a single parent. It was the only thing I knew, but it was the most interesting, exciting thing I could do. I wrote for newspapers. I worked on the BBC TV series and book *Claudia Roden's Mediterranean Cookery*. I went to every region of Italy for *The Sunday Times Magazine*'s "A Taste of Italy" and the book that followed. *The Book of Jewish Food* is about foods without terroir that Jews carried in their minds as baggage from one homeland to another. Researching it and *Arabesque*, about the cooking of Morocco, Turkey, and Lebanon and then *The Food of Spain* made me realize that food opens doors. While I was researching and recording traditional cuisines and spending time in home kitchens, I was inspired and learning from chefs who were experimenting and innovating and from those who were refining local traditions.

Working on this book, I revisited the tastes and joys of all the good times I've had and shared them with my family and my friends.

PLANNING A MEAL

A slice of the sun and sea for family and friends

The charm of a home-cooked meal is its casual simplicity. In the Mediterranean, with its traditions of hospitality, sociability, and conviviality, it is as much about the pleasures of the spirit as it is of the senses. Entertaining is a way of living that we can make our own. We may not all have the privilege of making food that is "from the landscape to the plate," but the majority of Mediterranean ingredients are readily available to us. They may not all be as good as those grown and ripened in the sun, but we can get the best out of them.

Preparing a meal for a crowd can be hard work, but it is always worth it, and planning the menu is part of the pleasure. These days I find it useful to ask if there is anything people can't eat. I always think of having a good variety of colors, flavors, textures, and nutrients with an emphasis on vegetables, pulses, and grains. It is sometimes a traditional three-course meal with a soup or vegetable starter, followed by a fish, chicken, meat, or vegetable main and a sweet. Alternatively, I'll put three or more dishes that complement each other on the table. This way of serving what restaurants call "sharing dishes" is appealing because people prefer variety above quantity. When it is just one person doing the cooking, it's not possible for them to cook too many different things and still enjoy the company. The art then is to choose, for at least part of the meal, something that is easy or that can be prepared in advance.

People are happy with a one-pot meal or a simple snack, even just a soup with bread, because you have cooked it for them. In the summer, for me, a snack might be a salad, a cold dish, or an omelet; in the winter it can be a heartwarming stew or a bake. If I have all the family over, it may be a large couscous. I love dessert, but sometimes just follow with cheese and fruit. With black coffee or mint tea, I serve chocolate or Medjool dates.

Have on the table some good bread, extra-virgin olive oil, flaky sea salt, a black pepper mill, and French piment d'Espelette and Aleppo pepper, known as pul biber. Both have a rich flavor and are less hot than other ground and crushed chiles.

Choose fresh, easy, robust wines that stand up to spices and chile, garlic, lemon, and sugar – well-chilled fruity whites, rosés, dry sherries, and sparkling wines for starters and fish and summer drinking; robust reds to go with lamb, pork, chicken, and also fish and cheese; a sweet wine, if you like, to serve with dessert. Keep a fine wine for the delicately flavored dishes. The Mediterranean is wine country. There are wonderful vibrant wines from Greece, Cyprus, Turkey, Lebanon, and Israel, but those from southern France, Italy, and Spain are more readily available and affordable. Spirits distilled from grapes – in particular anise-flavored pastis in France, and arak, raki, and ouzo in the eastern Mediterranean – are commonly served with chilled water (which turns them cloudy white) and ice as aperitifs and are also imbibed throughout the meal in the eastern Mediterranean. Beer is a good warm-weather drink, especially if you are eating outdoors. We love making sangria for a barbecue.

APPETIZERS

The pleasure of savoring bits of food with drinks in a relaxed way in convivial company is one of the joys of Mediterranean life. It is a tradition, a ritual, and an institution that was born in the world of bars, taverns, and cafés. But at home, too, there are traditions of hospitality where people offer something to eat with a drink.

The appetizers I grew up with are Middle Eastern mezze. When my father came home from work, we would sit on the balcony where we could see felukas (sailboats) gliding gracefully on the Nile, and Awad, our cook, would bring a tray of little things to eat. My parents had a glass of arak or whisky and nibbled at the food – feta cheese, hummus, olives, pickles, radishes, and the like – while we children would wolf it down before being stopped by Mother because we were having dinner soon. When my parents entertained their friends to play cards, every space in the apartment was filled with rented card tables, and a buffet included an enormous array of mezze.

I was always intrigued by the fantastical stories relatives told of a place called Zahlé, a mountain vacation resort in the Bekaa Valley in Lebanon, where they ate an incredible variety of fabulous mezze. That mythical place stayed in my mind and in my dreams, so you can imagine my excitement when, a few years ago, I found myself stopping in Zahlé for a mezze lunch on the way back to Beirut from a wedding near Baalbeck. Fergus Henderson of London's St. John restaurant was at the wedding with his extended family, and I got a lift with his parents and sister and painter Ffiona Lewis. The menu was huge. I wished I could try everything. While I took notes of what we ate, Ffiona sketched the empty plates with remnants of food after we finished. A year later, she exhibited the resulting paintings (they are great) at a London gallery.

Zahlé is now a town full of concrete housing overlooked by a giant statue of the Virgin Mary perched on the mountainside. There are vineyards around and arak is produced. According to legend, this is where the Arab mezze was born, in 1920, when the first two cafés opened by the river and started serving mountain village foods with the local arak. Gradually, the entire valley became filled with open-air cafés, each larger and more luxurious than the next, each vying with ever more varied mezze to attract customers who flocked from all over the Middle East.

What I learned in Zahlé and elsewhere in the eastern Mediterranean and North Africa has inspired some of the dishes that I serve as a first course. What I serve with drinks I have learned from people at home, usually purées or pastes on little toasts or as dips, whose rich, strong flavors are meant to open the appetite. When you have a whole meal to prepare, you don't have time for elaborate appetizers. I always have something in the fridge, such as salami or other charcuterie, some cheese to cut up, and some olives and nuts, if someone should be around unexpectedly for a drink.

FOCACCIA

Of all the Mediterranean breads, focaccia (*fugassa* in the local dialect) – one of the great triumphs of Ligurian cooking – is the easiest to make at home. In Liguria, every seaside resort has its own version. The best I've eaten was in Genoa. Whenever I make it, I can't stop eating it.

Serve it cut into small squares as an antipasto and try the classic variations on page 32.

Serves 6 to 8

1 tbsp instant (fast-acting) yeast
1 pinch sugar
2 cups / 480ml lukewarm water
5⅓ cups / 735g bread flour
2½ tsp salt
5 tbsp / 75ml extra-virgin olive oil, plus more for drizzling

Dissolve the yeast and sugar in about ½ cup / 120ml of the warm water and let sit for about 10 minutes until it froths.

In a large bowl, mix the flour and salt and make a well in the center. Pour in the yeast mixture and 3 tbsp of the olive oil and stir with a wooden spoon. Add the remaining 1½ cups / 360ml warm water very gradually – adding just enough to make a soft ball that holds together, mixing first with the wooden spoon, then working it in with your hand.

Turn the dough onto a lightly floured surface and knead for about 10 minutes, until very smooth and elastic (adding a little flour if too sticky, or a drop of water if too dry).

Drizzle a little oil into the bowl and turn the dough in it to coat it all over. Cover the bowl with a clean tea towel and let rise in a warm place for about 1½ hours, or until doubled in bulk.

Oil one or two baking pans: I use two round 11-inch pans, but a large rectangular one will do very well.

Knead the dough very briefly to punch out the air, then flatten into your oiled baking pans, pressing it down with oiled hands. As the dough is very elastic and will spring back, you may need to stretch it again a few times. A focaccia can be thick or thin, so the flattened dough can be ¼ to ⅜ inch thick. Cover with the towel or foil and let rise again in a warm place for about 45 minutes.

continued

Preheat the oven to 425°F.

Just before baking, use your fingers to make deep holes all over the dough and drizzle or brush with the remaining 2 tbsp olive oil.

Bake the focaccia, one pan at a time, for 20 to 30 minutes, or until crisp and golden on top and cooked through. It is best eaten warm, cut into wedges or squares.

Variations (before baking)

~ Sprinkle 1½ tsp coarse sea salt over the top.

~ Sprinkle with two or three chopped garlic cloves and the needles of two rosemary sprigs or 2 tbsp chopped sage leaves.

~ Sprinkle with 1 tbsp chopped oregano and a scant ½ cup / 75g pitted black olives, finely chopped.

~ Brush with 3 tbsp tapenade (see page 34).

~ Fry two sliced large onions in 3 tbsp olive oil over very low heat for about 45 minutes, until very soft, covering the pan to begin with and stirring occasionally. You may also let the onions brown and caramelize if you wish. Scatter over the top of the dough.

~ Pluck three red piquillo peppers from a jar, cut into ribbons, and scatter over the dough along with three chopped garlic cloves.

TARAMA

One of the joys of my days as an art student in London was dipping into a bowl of tarama with a piece of pita at a Cypriot café on Charlotte Street, called The Black Cat. It was one of a very few places where I could eat the foods of my childhood.

Tarama can be magnificent, but you must find a good source and buy really good-quality smoked cod roe. The best type that I buy from my fishmonger is loose and pinky beige and the resulting creamy dip is ivory-colored, not pink. I have tried the roes that are more readily available, which come vacuum-packed, look flattened, and are dark orangey brown, but they have been too salty and oversmoked. You can improve on them by soaking them in water for 2 hours, changing the water a couple of times. This will also make them easier to skin.

When my family gets together these days, we rely on my son Simon to make the tarama. His is always marvelous, with a delicate fishy flavor, because he has a good source for the roe. This is his recipe, but he makes it to taste and keeps adding olive oil and lemon juice until satisfied.

Serve it as a dip with warmed pita bread, cut into triangles with scissors, or thin toast.

Serves 8

9½ oz / 270g smoked cod roe

2 small garlic cloves, crushed

5 tbsp / 75ml lemon juice, or more to taste

7 tbsp / 100ml sunflower oil

2 tbsp extra-virgin olive oil, or more to taste

Skin the smoked cod roe, if it's easy to do so (I don't always manage to get all the skin off and it's fine). Put it in a food processor, add the garlic and lemon juice, and blend until smooth.

Gradually add the sunflower oil and olive oil in a thin trickle while the blades are running and blend to the consistency of a thick mayonnaise. Taste and add more lemon juice or olive oil, if you like.

Scrape the tarama into a bowl, cover, and chill in the fridge, where it will firm up, before serving.

TAPENADE

Traveling south in France, I felt, at a certain point, that I had opened a door into another world. The sky was different, the light and colors and smells were different, the architecture and vegetation were different – and there were olive trees. This famous paste consists mostly of olives but takes its name from the old Provençal word for caper, *tapeno*. It is the ideal appetizer, but you must use good-quality olives such as Kalamata, which are now readily available, pitted, in jars. The rum or brandy makes it special. Spread it on toast or serve as a dip. I use any left over as a sauce for pasta.

Serves 8 to 10

5¾ oz / 160g good-quality pitted black olives, such as Kalamata

2 tbsp capers in brine, squeezed

3 anchovy fillets in oil, drained

1 garlic clove, crushed (optional)

3 tbsp rum or brandy, to taste (optional)

2 to 3 tbsp extra-virgin olive oil

Using an immersion blender, blend together the olives, capers, anchovies, garlic (if using), rum or brandy (if using), and olive oil to form a smooth paste. It keeps in the fridge for up to 2 weeks.

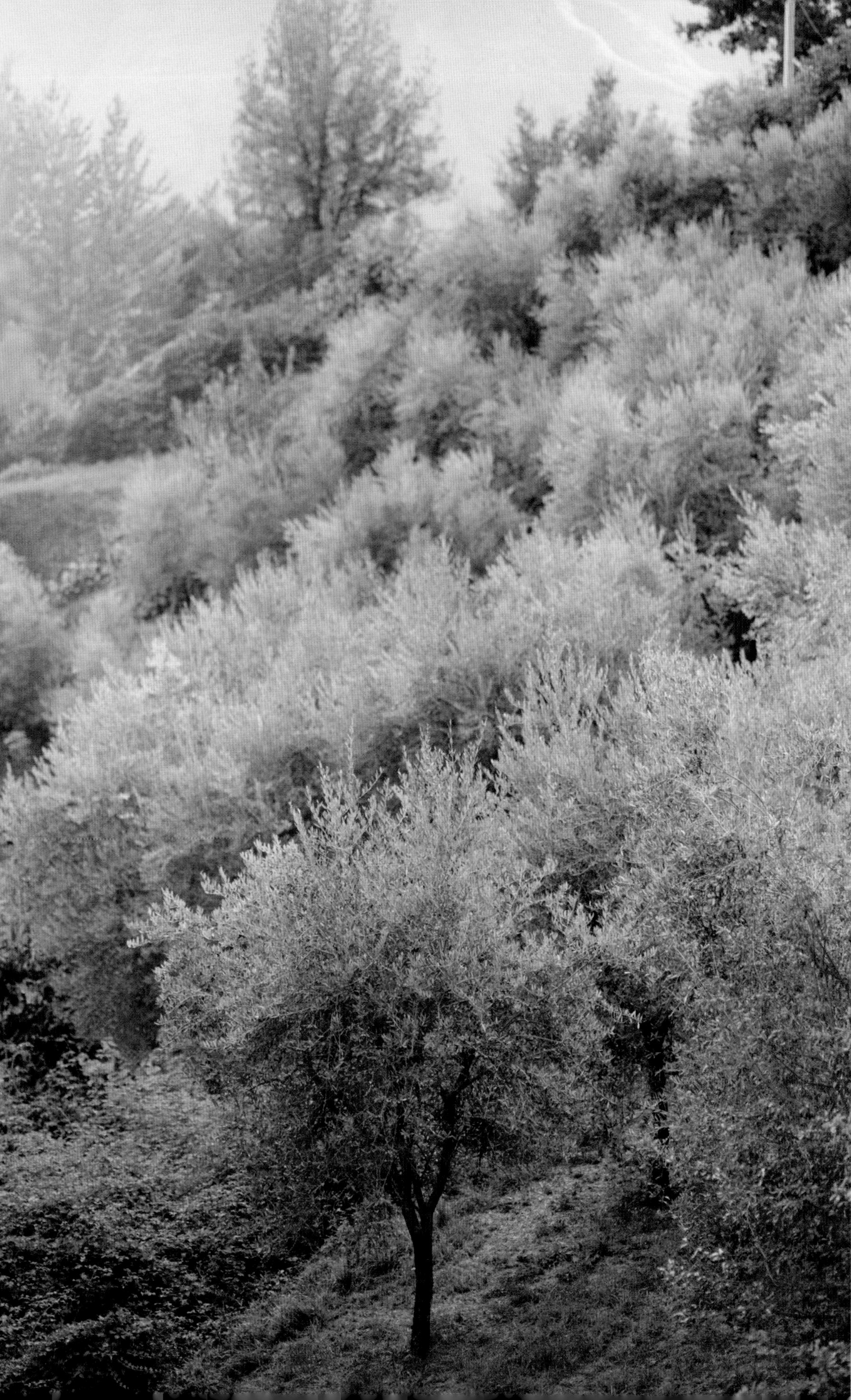

FRESH GOAT CHEESE WITH HERBS AND OLIVES

One summer, when my children were small, we camped at Lacoste in the Vaucluse in the South of France. My art school friend, the late Dutch sculptor Ans Hey, was building a house on the side of a hill with the help of her Amsterdam colleagues and students. I helped with the cooking. The area was blanketed with a scrub full of fragrant wild herbs. Every day, the children were sent off to gather some to throw in the fire under a huge grill where meat was roasting, or to put in a salad, omelet, or stew. We would mash some into the fresh goat cheeses we bought at the weekly farmers' markets, sometimes adding a little of the pastis we were drinking.

At home in London, I use other anise-flavored spirits such as arak, or sometimes rum. I buy alcoholic spirits mainly for cooking. It is worth investing in a few as they have an important place in northern Mediterranean cooking.

Serve on toast or as a dip for sticks of raw vegetables, such as cucumber or carrot.

Serves 8 to 10

5 oz / 140g fresh goat cheese

1½ tbsp extra-virgin olive oil

1 tbsp anise-flavored spirit such as pastis, arak, raki, or ouzo or white rum (optional)

1 small garlic clove, crushed (optional)

black pepper

1 tbsp snipped fresh chives or dill

5 pitted black olives, chopped

Using a fork, mash the goat cheese with the olive oil and anise-flavored spirit or rum and garlic (if using) and season with a little pepper.

Garnish with a sprinkling of chives or dill and the olives before serving.

Pictured at center front on page 34.

MUHAMMARA WALNUT AND ROASTED PEPPER DIP

This dip can be mild, as it is in Syria, or very hot with lots of chiles, as I had it in Gaziantep in Turkey. The city of Gaziantep was once part of Syria, where my great-grandfather Haham Abraham ha Cohen Douek was a young rabbi (in what was then Antep) before he became Chief Rabbi of Aleppo. I keep a portrait of him in my kitchen, in a kaftan and turban and wearing the medals pinned on him by Sultan Abdul Hamid II. When my family moved to Cairo, they brought the tastes of Aleppo with them.

My own version is very easy to make, using a jar of roasted and peeled piquillo peppers from Spain, which you will find in supermarkets. Garnish the muhammara, if you like, with walnut halves or pomegranate seeds. Serve it on toast or in Little Gem lettuce leaves.

Serves 8

one 12-oz / 340g jar red piquillo peppers

3½ oz / 100g walnut halves

1 slice whole-wheat bread, crusts removed

2 garlic cloves, crushed

1 to 1½ tbsp pomegranate molasses

juice of ½ lemon

3 to 4 tbsp extra-virgin olive oil

1½ tsp ground cumin

¼ to ½ tsp Aleppo pepper or piment d'Espelette

salt

Drain the piquillos well and put them in a food processor with the walnuts, bread, garlic, molasses, lemon juice, olive oil, cumin, and Aleppo pepper or piment d'Espelette. Season with salt and blend to a thick, coarse paste.

Spread the paste in a shallow dish to serve.

EGGPLANT PURÉE

I love the creamy flesh and slightly bitter, smoky taste of roasted eggplants with just olive oil and lemon. It is for good reason that in France it is known as *caviar d'aubergines*. Variations of this purée are found all around the Mediterranean. Serve it as a dip or spread on toast.

Serves 4 to 6

extra-virgin olive oil for brushing, plus ¼ cup / 60ml

3 eggplants, trimmed and cut in half lengthwise

juice of ½ to 1 lemon, or more to taste

salt and black pepper

Preheat the broiler to high. Line a baking sheet with foil, brush it with olive oil, and add the eggplants, cut-side down. Broil for 20 to 25 minutes, until the skins are black and blistered and the eggplants feel very soft inside when you press them. (Alternatively, preheat the oven to 425°F, prick the whole eggplants in a few places with a pointed knife so they don't burst, and roast them for about 45 minutes, turning them at least once.)

When the eggplants are cool enough to handle, use a spoon to scoop out the flesh into a colander and gently press to get rid of some of the juices. Chop the flesh with a sharp knife and then mash it with a fork.

In a bowl, beat the ¼ cup / 60ml olive oil with the lemon juice, season with salt and pepper, and mix in the mashed eggplants before serving.

Variations

~ For Levantine baba ghanouj, beat ¼ cup / 75g tahini with 2 tbsp water and the juice of 1 lemon (the tahini stiffens at first, then softens), then beat in the mashed eggplants. Season with salt and pepper and add one or two crushed garlic cloves. Before serving, stir in 2 tbsp chopped flat-leaf parsley.

~ For Turkish buran, mix the mashed eggplants with 1 cup / 240g Greek yogurt, the juice of 1 lemon, and a crushed garlic clove, then season with salt.

~ For a Syrian version, mix the mashed eggplants with 2 tbsp pomegranate molasses, 1 tbsp lemon juice, and 2 tbsp extra-virgin olive oil, then season with salt and pepper.

~ For a spicy Moroccan version, add a crushed garlic clove, a good pinch of piment d'Espelette, ½ tsp ground cumin, and 1 tbsp chopped cilantro leaves.

LABNEH

This thick, velvety drained yogurt makes a wonderfully refreshing side dish. There are few things it doesn't go with. It is my little luxury to eat it, without salt, just by itself. A traditional way of draining the yogurt is to hang it in a long cloth set over a bowl, but I leave it in a colander. I serve it as a mezze with a drizzle of extra-virgin olive oil and a sprinkle of sumac, Aleppo pepper, crushed garlic, dried mint, grated lemon zest, snipped fresh chives, or chopped dill – not all at once. Serve it with warmed triangles of pita bread or sticks of raw cucumber and carrot.

Serves 8

16 oz / 450g Greek yogurt

¼ tsp fine sea salt (optional)

Line a colander with a clean cloth (such as a napkin or a piece of cheesecloth) and place it in a bowl so that it doesn't touch the bottom. Pour in the yogurt, beat in the salt (if you want it salty), and bring up the corners of the cloth to cover it.

Put the bowl in the fridge and let it sit overnight, or longer. The liquid whey will drain away; you will have to pour it out occasionally. The longer you leave it, the thicker the labneh gets.

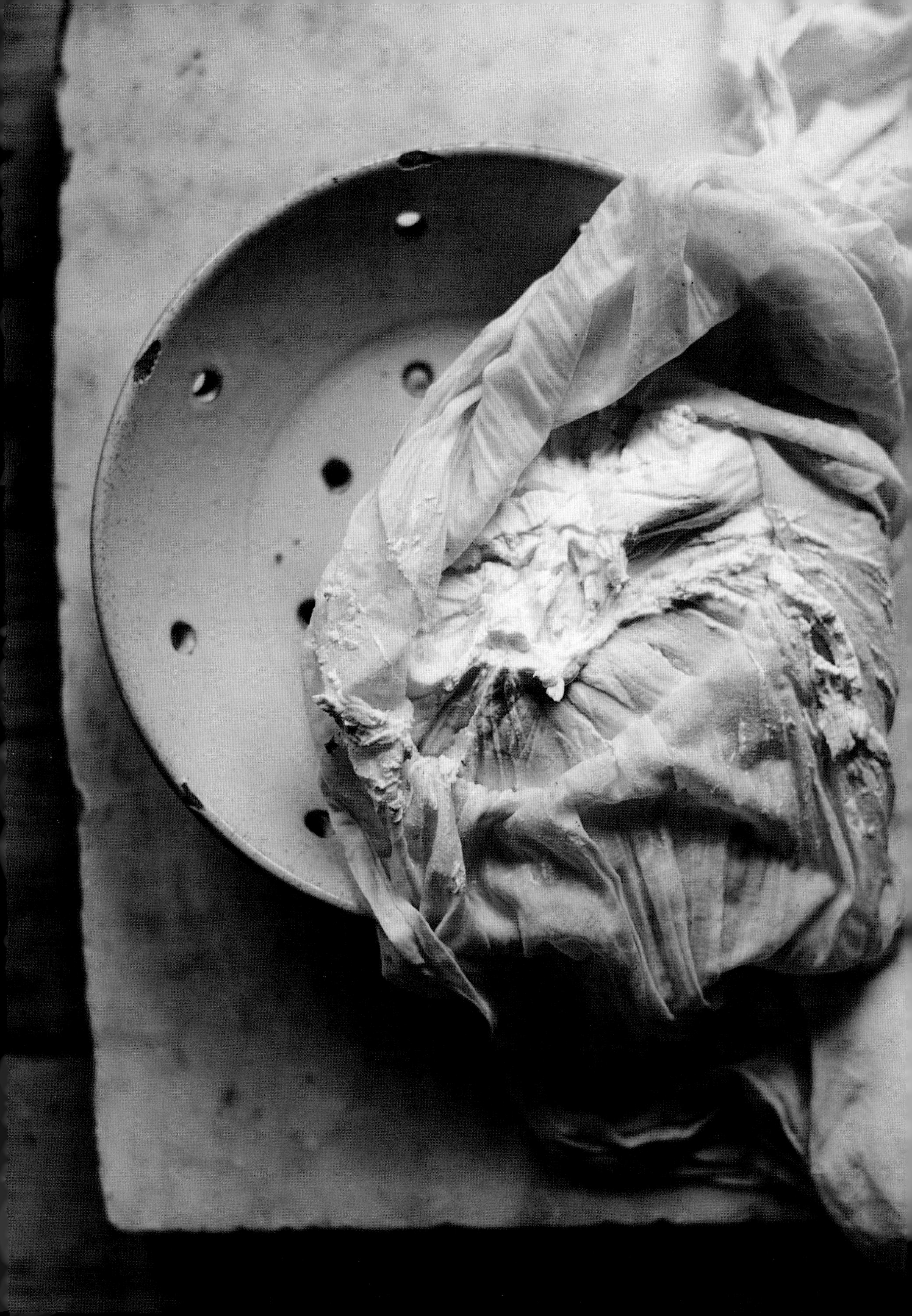

ROASTED CHEESE POLENTA CUBES

It is amazing how polenta keeps reinventing itself. Originally the despised porridge of a desperately poor northern Italian peasantry, it appeared in restaurants in the 1980s as a thin, grilled triangle or as a creamy base for elegant food. I can never make enough of these heavenly bites, crisp and golden on the outside and soft inside. Everyone adores them. You can make the polenta the day before, then cut it into cubes and roast them just before serving. My son Simon has adopted these as a side dish for, say, sausages, in which case the cubes should be cut a little bigger.

Makes about 32 cubes

olive oil or sunflower oil for brushing, plus ¼ cup / 60ml

4 cups / 950ml water

2 tsp salt

1¾ cups / 250g instant polenta

2½ oz / 75g Parmesan or Grana Padano, grated

3½ oz / 100g semisoft cheese such as Fontina or Taleggio, cut into pieces

1 tbsp chopped rosemary leaves

black pepper

Line an 8 x 12-inch baking pan with foil – if you have a larger pan, line it with foil that you can fold up to contain the polenta in a layer about 1 inch thick. Brush with oil.

Bring the water and salt to a boil in a very large saucepan. Pour in the polenta, whisking vigorously. When it comes back to a boil, lower the heat and continue to stir with the whisk for 3 minutes, making sure that no lumps form. It will gurgle and splatter, so you might need to put a cloth around your hand. Add both cheeses, the rosemary, and some pepper and whisk well to make sure the cheese melts evenly. Cover the pan and cook over very low heat for 8 minutes, stirring occasionally.

Pour the polenta into the prepared pan, let it cool, then cover and refrigerate for 2 hours.

Half an hour before serving, preheat the oven to 475°F.

Cut the polenta into cubes with a sharp knife. Pour the ¼ cup / 60ml oil into another, larger, baking dish or roasting pan, and tip the polenta cubes into it, then turn them in the oil to coat on all sides. Roast for 20 to 25 minutes, until nicely crisp and golden, turning them over once. Serve hot.

GREEN OLIVE, WALNUT, AND POMEGRANATE SALAD

This little salad, a thrilling mix of flavors, textures, and colors that is almost too glorious to look at, is a specialty of Gaziantep, a Turkish city on the border with Syria, famous for its gastronomy. If you don't have pomegranate seeds, it's still delicious.

Serves 4

generous ½ cup / 100g good-quality pitted green olives in brine, drained

½ cup / 50g walnuts

3 green onions, chopped

1 bunch flat-leaf parsley, leaves chopped

2 tbsp extra-virgin olive oil

1 tbsp lemon juice

2 tbsp pomegranate molasses

salt

piment d'Espelette, to taste

3 tbsp pomegranate seeds

Coarsely chop the olives and walnuts, place in a serving dish, and mix with the green onions and parsley.

In a small bowl, mix the olive oil, lemon juice, and pomegranate molasses with a little salt and piment d'Espelette. Pour over the olives and walnuts and sprinkle with the pomegranate seeds before serving.

CHICKEN LIVER MOUSSE

A tiny tartlet filled with an exquisite chicken liver mousse was part of an assortment of Alain Ducasse's canapés that I was offered when I interviewed the great chef at his Michelin 3-star restaurant in Paris. The sweet and fortified wines give mine a sumptuous flavor. I serve it on lightly toasted brioche bread, sometimes with a teaspoon of fruit preserves such as quince or apricot beside it.

Serves 6

14 oz / 400g chicken livers
2 tbsp unsalted butter
2 garlic cloves, crushed
1 tsp thyme leaves
salt and black pepper
¼ cup / 60ml sweet Marsala or muscatel wine
2 tbsp brandy or ruby port
7 tbsp / 100ml heavy cream

Chicken livers are generally sold cleaned, but check them over and trim off any sinews or greenish bits.

Melt the butter in a large skillet over high heat, add the livers, and cook for 2 minutes. Add the garlic and thyme, season with salt and pepper, and cook, turning the livers until browned all over but still a little bloody inside. Pour in the Marsala or muscatel and let it bubble and evaporate over medium heat for a minute or so – the chicken livers should still be pink inside.

Tip the livers with the pan juices into a food processor, add the brandy or port, and blend to a paste. Using a whisk, whip the cream until thick, then add it to the food processor and blend to a creamy consistency. Taste and adjust the seasoning. Scrape into a bowl, cover, and refrigerate for 3 hours before serving.

BANCA NAZIONALE DEL LAVORO
BNL

SOUPS

When I first moved into my little studio in Paris, in the long cobbled courtyard that had once been stables, the first thing I did was buy pots and pans and kitchen utensils. I went to the flea market and bought a small country table (they called it a wine-tasting table) and four wooden chairs. It was 1989. I phoned relatives and friends and started inviting people over to eat. I took my basket on wheels to the Rue Cler street market, filled it with goodies, and went home to cook. I was ecstatic. But I soon stopped making dinners in my tiny kitchen because I wanted to be out and about meeting friends, researching at libraries, seeing exhibitions, browsing in bookshops, going to events. Paris is a city where so much is going on and it feels good just to wander around the streets. The name of a street, the sight of a restaurant or a café, brought back memories of the times we came on vacation with my parents and when I was at school. I would sit in a café, order a coffee or a soup, read my paper, and dream.

Soup is everyone's comfort food, and it is mine. At one time, I took lunch breaks in a little restaurant that specialized in healthful vegetarian food. Every day they made a different cream of vegetable soup, a velouté de légumes, which could be pumpkin, carrots, leeks, mushrooms, cauliflower, peas. In the past, they might have forced the soup through a food mill, now they blend it in a food processor. Some are nostalgic for the old way.

When I asked a sociologist friend about the cuisines des terroirs, he said "They exist only in cookery books." You might not find regional dishes in their regions, but I have found them in Paris, in bistros and restaurants, and in people's homes. Much of the population of the capital comes from the regions and some keep up family traditions.

When I first came to Paris, the food of the Midi (Southern France) was not valued. It was even despised and considered not properly French, because there were so many foreign influences: Spanish, Arab, Italian. However, now it is the most popular for its strong flavors, spices, and perfumes and its use of olive oil. It is what people want to eat and the inspiration for influential avant-garde chefs such as Alain Ducasse. La cuisine du soleil, also called la cuisine des épices, is in its golden age.

When I started thinking of soups for this book, I went through all the ones I had eaten and loved around the Mediterranean, for inspiration. There were many. What you have here are my favorites. They make an easy and delightful first course. You will find splendid fish soups, which are the heart and soul of the Mediterranean, in the Seafood and Shellfish chapter.

GAZPACHO ANDALUZ

This is the best thing you can have in the summer, when tomatoes are sweet and full of flavor. When I stayed with Manolo el Sereno in Frailes, a village in Andalusia, I helped him make enough gazpacho to fill half a dozen giant Coca-Cola bottles. He told me of the time when, from the age of seven, he worked on an estate, looking after the mules and helping to make food for the seasonal laborers. When they worked in the vegetable gardens, they took dornillos (large mortars) to pound the ingredients for gazpacho, along with olive oil, salt, vinegar, and some bread. Manolo was the president of the gastronomic guild of the province of Jaén. It was their festival, and everyone brought food. A band played flamenco and people got up to sing of the pain and joys of those who once worked on the land.

Serves 6 to 8

1 slice of good white bread, crusts removed (optional)

2¼ lb / 1kg ripe plum tomatoes

1 green or red bell pepper, seeded and cut into pieces

1 cucumber, peeled and cut into pieces

2 garlic cloves, crushed

3 tbsp sherry vinegar or wine vinegar, or more to taste

¼ cup / 60ml extra-virgin olive oil, plus 3 tbsp

1 tsp sugar, or more to taste

salt and black pepper

If using the bread, preheat the broiler to low and put the bread under the broiler to dry out without browning it, turning once. Break it up into pieces.

Wash the tomatoes, then quarter them and remove the little white hard bits at the stem end.

Blend the bell pepper to a paste in a food processor (a green pepper gives a more zingy flavor, a red one is sweeter). Add the bread, tomatoes, cucumber, garlic, vinegar, ¼ cup / 60ml olive oil, and sugar; season with salt and black pepper; and blend to a light creamy consistency. Pour into a serving bowl, cover, and chill in the fridge for 1 hour.

Check the seasoning and serve in soup bowls. Drizzle each serving with a bit of the remaining 3 tbsp olive oil.

YOGURT SOUP WITH ORZO AND CHICKPEAS

This splendid, delicately flavored soup is inspired by one that charmed me completely at a dinner in Istanbul to celebrate the adoption by UNESCO of Gaziantep as a Creative City for its gastronomy. All the recipes on the menu hailed from the city. You must try it – it's marvelous. My granddaughter Ruby, who tested it, has adopted it with her friends at college. She sent me a photo of them eating it at their kitchen table with antique candlesticks and a bottle of wine.

The egg yolk and cornstarch prevent the yogurt from curdling as it cooks. The tiny pasta called orzo (or you can use long-grain rice) is cooked separately and added just before serving – if left in the soup too long it becomes bloated and mushy.

Serves 4

¼ cup / 50g orzo or long-grain rice

3 cups / 720ml chicken or vegetable stock

1 tbsp cornstarch

1 egg yolk

1 cup / 240g Greek yogurt

1 tbsp dried mint

1 good pinch saffron threads, or ½ tsp ground turmeric

black pepper

¾ cup / 120g canned chickpeas, drained and rinsed

salt

extra-virgin olive oil for serving

sumac for serving

Aleppo pepper for serving

Cook the orzo or rice in boiling salted water for about 10 minutes, until done (check the package instructions), and then drain. At the same time, bring the stock to a boil in a separate pan.

In a bowl, beat the cornstarch and egg yolk together with a fork until smooth, then beat in a spoonful of the yogurt until well blended. You can then add the remaining yogurt and beat until combined. Stir in the mint, saffron or turmeric, and some black pepper.

Take the stock off the heat and pour in the yogurt mixture, whisking vigorously. Stir over very low heat until the soup begins to simmer. Continue to stir for 3 to 5 minutes, until it thickens slightly, then add the chickpeas and heat through. Season with a little salt.

A few minutes before serving, mix the cooked orzo or rice into the soup.

Serve with extra-virgin olive oil, sumac, and Aleppo pepper for people to sprinkle on the soup if they want to.

CHILLED CREAM OF BEET AND YOGURT SOUP

This wonderfully refreshing and tasty electric-pink soup is inspired by a Turkish salad. The earthy sweetness of the beets marries well with the slightly tart creamy yogurt. You must use fresh young beets that are sold in bunches with their leaves on.

Serves 6 to 8

6 medium beets (about 1 lb 10 oz / 750g total weight)

3 cups / 720ml water

1½ cups / 360g plain whole-milk yogurt, plus more for dolloping

juice of 1 lemon

salt

4 tbsp chopped fresh dill or chives

Wash the beets and cut off the leaves, then peel them, cut in half, and put in a large pan with the water. Bring to a boil, then simmer, with the lid on, for 30 to 40 minutes, until very tender. Let cool and then blend in a food processor until smooth.

Add the yogurt and lemon juice to the processor, season with salt, and blend to a light creamy consistency.

Serve the soup dolloped with yogurt and sprinkled with the dill or chives.

CREAM OF GREEN PEA SOUP WITH PISTOU

My Mediterranean addition to this homely, velvety soup is a drizzle of Provençal sauce pistou, the French version of the pesto found across the border in Liguria. It adds flavor and richness. When I make this, I think of my friend the late Mireille Johnston, who presented BBC TV series *A Cook's Tour of France* in the early 1990s. She lived with her husband and two daughters around the corner from my little studio in Paris. She would call and say "On t'attend pour la soupe" ("we're expecting you for the soup") – *la soupe* was an entire meal. She was born in Nice and had a special love for what she called the "cuisine of the sun."

Serves 4

Pistou

1 bunch basil, leaves only

1 to 1½ garlic cloves, crushed

1½ oz / 40g Parmesan, grated

3 tbsp extra-virgin olive oil

2 tbsp olive oil

1 onion, chopped

2 garlic cloves, chopped

3 cups / 390g frozen peas

2½ cups / 590ml chicken or vegetable stock

7 tbsp / 100ml heavy cream

salt and black pepper

For the pistou, using an immersion blender, blend together the basil, garlic, Parmesan, and extra-virgin olive oil to make a thick paste. Set aside.

Warm the 2 tbsp olive oil in a pan over medium heat. Add the onion and garlic and fry, stirring often, for 3 to 4 minutes, until softened.

Add the frozen peas and stock to the pan and bring to a boil. Lower the heat and simmer for 7 to 10 minutes, until the peas are soft.

Add the cream to the pan, then blend the soup with an immersion blender and season with salt and pepper. Reheat if necessary and add 1 tbsp or so of pistou to each serving.

EGYPTIAN RED LENTIL SOUP

I traveled along the Nile to research the peasant food and to interview chefs in tourist hotels before a seminar I was giving for the Egyptian Chefs Association. In a little village, seeing me walk past her house, a woman invited me in and offered me lentil soup. It was the type of spicy, creamy comfort food that I love. Later, at the seminar in the ballroom of the Marriott Hotel (a former palace in the Zamalek district of Cairo, where I used to live), I told the chefs to put lentil soup on their menus.

Serves 6 to 8

1 large onion, chopped
1 carrot, finely chopped
4 to 5 garlic cloves, finely chopped
3 tbsp olive oil
1½ cups / 300g split red lentils
8½ cups / 2L chicken or vegetable stock
1½ to 2 tsp ground cumin
1½ tsp ground coriander
1 good pinch Aleppo pepper (optional)
juice of 1 lemon
salt and black pepper

Soften the onion, carrot, and garlic in the olive oil in a large pan over low heat for about 10 minutes.

Add the lentils and stock to the pan, bring to a boil, and then skim off the foam that forms at the top. Simmer for 30 to 40 minutes, until the lentils have disintegrated.

Stir in the cumin, coriander, Aleppo pepper (if using), and lemon juice and season with salt and black pepper. Simmer for 5 minutes more. If the soup needs thinning – it should not be too thick – add a little water and bring to a boil again. Serve hot.

Caramelized onion garnish (optional)

In a large skillet, fry two or three large sliced onions in 3 to 4 tbsp olive oil or sunflower oil, covered, over low heat for 20 to 30 minutes, stirring often, until they are very soft. Remove the lid, turn the heat to medium, and cook, stirring often, for about 15 minutes, until the onions are really dark brown and caramelized. Add a good 1 tbsp to each serving of soup.

EGG AND LEMON CHICKEN SOUP

My version of sharp, creamy Greek avgolemono soup is a light meal in itself, with chunks of chicken and rice or orzo. Using chicken with bone and skin gives it a little fat and more flavor. You can prepare the soup in advance and whisk in the egg-lemon mixture just before serving. Serve the rice separately so that people can say how much of it they want in the soup.

Serves 4

4 cups / 950ml good chicken stock
3 fat chicken thighs, bone-in, skin-on
salt and black pepper
⅓ cup / 125g long-grain rice or orzo
2 eggs
3 tbsp lemon juice
1 tbsp finely chopped flat-leaf parsley

Put the stock and chicken thighs in a large pan. Set over high heat, bring to a boil, skim off the foam that forms at the top, season with salt and pepper, and then turn the heat to low, cover, and simmer for about 25 minutes, until the thighs are very tender. Lift them out and let sit until cool enough to handle. Remove the skin and bones, cut the meat into largish pieces, and put it back into the stock.

In another pan, bring plenty of salted water to a boil and add the rice or orzo. Cook for 10 to 15 minutes, until done (check the package instructions), and then drain quickly.

Just before you are ready to serve, return the stock to a simmer. Beat the eggs vigorously in a bowl, then beat in the lemon juice. Gradually add two ladlefuls of the simmering soup, beating constantly. Pour this back into the soup, beating vigorously. Take the soup off the heat quickly or the eggs will curdle.

Serve the soup garnished with the parsley.

PUMPKIN SOUP WITH ORZO AND AMARETTI

The pumpkins of the city of Mantua in northern Italy (called *capello del prete* because they look like a priest's hat) are celebrated for their exceptionally sweet and delicate flavor, and the city is famous for its pumpkin risotti and tortelli. This soup is inspired by the filling in the tortelli di zucca that I ate there. If you don't have a fine-tasting pumpkin, use butternut squash.

You can prepare the soup in advance, but cook the pasta separately when reheating the soup and add it just before serving.

Serves 6 to 8

1¾ lb / 800g pumpkin or butternut squash, peeled, seeded, and cut into pieces

2¼ cups / 530ml water

2 chicken or vegetable bouillon cubes

¾ cup / 150g orzo

2 cups / 480ml whole milk

salt and black pepper

ground cinnamon for sprinkling

grated Parmesan for sprinkling

9 crunchy (not chewy) amaretti biscuits, roughly crushed

Put the pumpkin or squash in a large saucepan with the water and bouillon cubes. Bring to a boil, then simmer, covered, over low heat for 20 minutes, until the pumpkin is soft.

At the same time, cook the orzo in boiling salted water for about 10 minutes, until al dente, and then drain quickly.

Blend the pumpkin or squash to a purée using an immersion blender (or in a food processor), then add the milk. Bring to a simmer, taking care not to let it boil over, and season with salt and pepper.

Just before serving, bring the soup to a simmer and add the cooked orzo. Pass around little bowls of cinnamon, grated Parmesan, and crumbled amaretti for your guests to sprinkle over their soup.

SALADS AND COLD VEGETABLE DISHES

A fresh leaf salad with fruit and perhaps a soft goat cheese is a delightful way to start a meal. Vegetables cooked in oil to be served cold, a culinary style of the Mediterranean, also make a perfect first course. The advantage, for me, is that they can be made in advance, and any leftovers can be offered from the fridge as an appetizer with drinks, a day or two later. I also make a casual summer meal of one or two cold vegetable dishes, accompanied by cheese or charcuterie and some good bread.

You can use various oils for cooking – I use olive oil or sunflower – but for dressing green salads and for drizzling on cooked vegetables, it has to be extra-virgin olive oil. For salad greens, I use a fruity, mild, delicate, fragrant extra virgin; to drizzle over cooked vegetables, depending on the vegetable, it can sometimes be a strong-tasting, bitter, spicy oil.

While hot vegetables are enhanced by herbs, cold vegetables and grain salads do well with spices, too, and with sharp or sweet-and-sour dressings and garnishes such as olives, capers, anchovies, nuts, and pomegranate seeds. In the Arab world, a certain magic surrounds the use of aromatics and spices, which are utilized for their flavor and are also believed to have medicinal, therapeutic, and even sometimes aphrodisiac value. In local folklore, they are variously believed to increase the appetite, help digestion, or calm the nerves, to be good for the heart and circulation, to be antitoxic or sexually stimulating, and even to kill microbes. Cumin is said to open the appetite, ginger to make people loving, rose water gives a rosy outlook, dill and aniseed have digestive qualities, and garlic is both health-giving and antiseptic – attributes that may be well founded or romantic. I used to bring back bags of spices and aromatics from souks and bazaars. Now, I find all that I need for cooking in London.

A taste that I love for cold vegetables is sweet-and-sour, obtained with lemon or vinegar and sugar or honey, or with pomegranate molasses. You find sweet-and-sour across the region. It is a legacy from medieval Baghdad. Chefs in Andalusia will tell you that it was introduced there by a lute player from Baghdad, known as Ziryab, who fled from the court of Harun al-Rashid and joined the court of Córdoba. When the Queen Elizabeth Hall at the Southbank Center in London put on a series of concerts called "Words and Music," they asked me to join a Spanish flamenco player and a lute player from Baghdad in an event they advertised as "A Night in Andalusia." I was to talk about my experiences of food in Andalusia between their pieces. I agreed with the flamenco player that I should talk about Ziryab, who is credited by musicians for introducing new music in Spain. *Ziryab* means "blackbird" – he had a dark complexion and is said to have sung like a bird. I think of him when I make eggplant in a spicy honey sauce (see page 106). Do try it.

Whenever you are after a sweet-and-sour or a savory-and-sweet taste, and when you are using spices and aromatics, it is best to start with little and then add more and adjust the balance after you taste, because ingredients vary as products of nature, and spices also depend on their age. Market brands also differ in strength for products such as rose and orange blossom waters and pomegranate molasses. Trust your taste. If you like something, then the flavoring is right.

CITRUS SALAD WITH GREENS

In Taormina, Sicily, I visited a ceramicist who had created a ceramic orchard of life-size orange and lemon trees. I still have the plates I bought from him and I have never forgotten the salad we ate sitting among the glittering trees. This salad is inspired by his. I serve it as a first course with bread, sometimes after a main course, or as part of a group of three or more "sharing" dishes that I put on the table together. It brings a tangy freshness to a meal.

The salad greens could be a mix of two or three varieties, some mild, some spicy or bitter, such as Little Gem lettuce leaves, pea shoots, lamb's lettuce, watercress, curly endive, or arugula. You could also toss some chopped herbs in with them.

Serves 6

1 large grapefruit

1 large sweet orange (a blood orange is nice)

6 oz / 170g baby salad greens

juice of ½ lemon

¼ cup / 60ml extra-virgin olive oil

salt and black pepper

1 good handful fresh mixed herbs such as chives, dill, and flat-leaf parsley, chopped

Using a serrated knife, slice off the tops of the grapefruit and orange, then cut down the sides, making sure you remove the pith with the peel. Then, cut the citrus into slices and arrange them on a wide platter.

Arrange the salad greens on top of the fruit. Mix together the lemon juice and olive oil, season with salt and pepper, and pour this dressing all over the salad. Sprinkle with the herbs before serving.

ARUGULA WITH PANCETTA AND GRAPES

I love the combination of hot, crisp, salty pancetta and soft, juicy, sweet grapes with the slightly bitter fresh leaves. You can fry the pancetta and grapes in advance and reheat them just before serving.

Serves 4 to 6

3 tbsp olive oil or sunflower oil

5 oz / 140g cubed pancetta

7 oz / 200g red or black grapes

3 cups / 65g arugula leaves

3 tbsp extra-virgin olive oil

1 tbsp lemon juice or white wine vinegar

salt and black pepper

Warm 1 tbsp of the oil in a small skillet over medium heat, add the pancetta, and fry for 8 to 10 minutes, stirring until the pancetta releases plenty of fat and becomes crisp. Drain on paper towels.

At the same time, warm the remaining 2 tbsp oil in another skillet over medium heat and fry the grapes, gently stirring, until they are soft and caramelized.

Spread the arugula leaves in a wide serving dish and dress with the extra-virgin olive oil, lemon juice or vinegar, and a sprinkling of salt and pepper. Scatter the grapes and pancetta over the salad before serving.

FENNEL WITH PEACHES AND FRESH GOAT CHEESE

The sweet taste and floral scent of peaches go very well with the creamy fresh goat cheese, fennel, and cucumber in this glorious salad. The peaches should be ripe but not soft – marinating them for an hour in the dressing will soften them. Put the other ingredients together at the last minute.

Serves 6 to 8

3 large orange-fleshed peaches
6 tbsp / 90ml extra-virgin olive oil
2 tbsp lemon juice
salt and black pepper
1 large fennel bulb, or 2 small ones
2 small cucumbers, peeled and sliced
8 oz / 225g mild soft fresh goat cheese, cut into 6 to 8 pieces

Drop the peaches into boiling water for a few seconds, then drain and let sit until cool enough to handle. Peel them, cut them in half, and then cut each half into three to six slices (depending on how many people you are serving), removing the pits. Put the peaches in a bowl.

In a small bowl, whisk together the olive oil and lemon juice and season with salt and pepper. Pour 2 tbsp of this dressing over the peaches and mix well. Let sit for about 1 hour, turning them in the dressing at least once before serving. Set the remaining dressing aside.

Trim the end(s) of the fennel bulb(s) and remove any tough outer leaves. Reserve any feathery fronds and cut the fennel into very thin, long slices using a sharp knife.

Just before serving, put the fennel and cucumber on a wide serving plate and toss with the remaining dressing. Add the peaches and goat cheese and pour in the juices from the peaches. Sprinkle on the feathery fennel fronds.

Variation

Instead of fennel, use a mixture of two or three of the following – lettuce, curly endive (frisée), lamb's lettuce, arugula.

CUCUMBER AND TOMATO SALAD

This is my simple everyday salad, as my mother always made it. If I have herbs in the fridge, I put some in. I sometimes add feta cheese.

Serves 4

4 small cucumbers, peeled and cut into ⅜-inch-thick slices, or 1 long one, peeled, cut in half lengthwise, and then sliced

5 plum tomatoes, cut into wedges

5 green onions, thinly sliced

3 tbsp extra-virgin olive oil

juice of ½ lemon

salt and black pepper

1 small handful fresh herbs such as flat-leaf parsley, oregano, dill, chives, chervil, and cilantro, chopped (optional)

3½ oz / 100g feta cheese, cut into chunks (optional)

Put the cucumbers, tomatoes, and green onions in a bowl.

In another bowl, whisk together the olive oil and lemon juice and season with salt and pepper to make a dressing.

Just before serving, pour the dressing over the salad and mix well. Sprinkle with the herbs and add the feta, if you like.

SWEET-AND-SOUR PEPERONATA

On my arrival in Palermo, as a guest of a cruise ship touring the Sicilian volcanic islands, the first dinner was in an aristocrat's ancient palazzo. The aristocrat's much younger Austrian wife sang operatic pieces. It was billed as a *monsu* dinner (the word is derived from "monsieur," for the French chefs who came to cook for the Sicilian aristocracy after the French Revolution). I have adopted their voluptuous peperonata in agrodolce and serve it as a first course or side dish or as an antipasto, spread on crostini.

Serves 4 to 6

3 large fleshy bell peppers (red, orange, yellow), seeded

5 tbsp / 75ml olive oil

2 red onions, halved and sliced

4 garlic cloves, peeled

salt and black pepper

1 tbsp sugar or honey

3 tbsp white or red wine vinegar

6 anchovy fillets in oil, drained (optional)

6 pitted black olives (optional)

1 tbsp drained capers (optional)

basil or mint sprigs, leaves torn (optional)

Cut the bell peppers into ribbons.

Warm the olive oil in a large skillet or sauté pan over low heat; add the onions, garlic, and bell peppers; season with salt and black pepper; and cook, covered, stirring occasionally, for 30 to 40 minutes, until they are very soft.

In a small bowl, stir to dissolve the sugar or honey in the vinegar. Pour over the vegetables and stir well. Cook for another 5 to 10 minutes.

Serve at room temperature. Garnish, if you like, with anchovy fillets, olives, and capers and sprinkle with basil or mint.

Postiglione Pietro

ZONA DI PRODUZIONE
CAT:
TARA gr.

RED PEPPER AND TOMATO SALAD

Inspired by Moroccan cooked salads, this one is a favorite for its glorious color and marvelous flavors. The addition of boiled lemon, with its unique sharp taste, is my little "fantasia."

Serves 4 to 6

3 large fleshy red bell peppers

1½ tbsp olive oil

10 oz / 285g cherry or baby plum tomatoes, such as Santini

½ to 1 fresh chile, seeded and chopped, or 1 good pinch piment d'Espelette (optional)

3 garlic cloves, finely chopped

½ tsp sugar

salt

1 small boiled lemon (see page 226), or ½ large one (optional)

3 to 4 tbsp extra-virgin olive oil

a few cilantro sprigs, leaves chopped

Preheat the oven to 425°F and line a baking sheet with parchment paper or foil. Cut the bell peppers in half through the stems; remove the stems, seeds, and membranes; and arrange the peppers, cut-side down, on the baking sheet. Roast for 25 to 35 minutes, until they are soft and their skin is blistered. Put them in an empty pan with a tight-fitting lid or in a bowl with a plate on top and let steam for 10 minutes, which will loosen the skins. When the peppers are cool enough to handle, peel off the skins and cut each half into four ribbons.

While the peppers are roasting, warm the olive oil in a skillet over low heat and add the tomatoes and chile or piment d'Espelette (if using). Cook for 10 minutes, shaking the pan and turning the tomatoes over with a spatula until they are soft. Push them to the side of the pan, add the garlic to an empty bit of the pan, and cook, stirring, until the aroma rises and the garlic just begins to color. Add the sugar and a sprinkle of salt and stir well.

Add the bell peppers to the tomatoes. If using the lemon, cut it into small pieces and add it to the pan, juice and all, but removing the seeds. Stir gently over low heat for a minute or so. Let cool.

Serve at room temperature, drizzled with the extra-virgin olive oil and sprinkled with cilantro.

Variations

- ~ Garnish with ten black olives and ten anchovy fillets in oil.
- ~ For Neapolitan peperoni e pomodorini in agrodolce, omit the sugar, boiled lemon, and cilantro. Dissolve 2 tbsp sugar in 7 tbsp / 100ml white wine vinegar, pour over the bell peppers and tomatoes, and cook for a minute or two.

SWEET-AND-SOUR MINTY GRILLED ZUCCHINI

Sweet-and-sour is one of the tastes the Arabs brought to Sicily in the ninth century. This zucchini dish, zucchine in agrodolce alla menta, is wonderful with whipped ricotta, which is given as a recommended option.

Serves 4

3 zucchini (about 1¾ lb / 800g total weight)

olive oil or sunflower oil for brushing

salt

7 tbsp / 100ml white wine vinegar

¼ cup / 50g sugar

1 tbsp dried mint

black pepper

extra-virgin olive oil for drizzling

Preheat the broiler to high. Line a baking sheet with foil.

Cut each zucchini lengthwise into ⅜-inch-thick slices. Place them on the foil, brush with oil on both sides, and sprinkle lightly with salt. Broil for about 10 minutes, turning them over once, until they are tender and lightly browned in places. Alternatively, you can cook them on a grill pan.

Warm the vinegar and sugar with the dried mint and some pepper in a small pan over medium heat, stirring until the sugar melts, then simmer for 2 minutes to reduce it a little. Arrange the zucchini slices side-by-side on a serving plate, pour the vinegar dressing over them, and add a drizzle of extra-virgin olive oil before serving.

Whipped ricotta

Using a fork, whip 1 cup / 240g ricotta with 1½ tbsp extra-virgin olive oil and the grated zest of ½ small lemon. Season with salt and pepper before serving.

MOZZARELLA SOAKED IN CREAM WITH BABY TOMATOES

In Italy in the 1980s, it was fashionable to call dishes *tricolore* after the green, white, and red Italian flag. There was risotto tricolore and pizza tricolore. The insalata di mozzarella e pomodori is still with us because tomatoes and basil are great with mozzarella. In this recipe, very fresh mozzarella di bufala is macerated in cream for a few hours to give a magical "burrata" effect. Sautéing the tomatoes gives them a sweet and intense flavor.

Serves 4 to 6

two 8-oz / 225g balls mozzarella di bufala, each cut into 6 slices

⅔ cup / 160ml heavy cream

salt and black pepper

1 lb / 450g red and yellow baby Santini tomatoes or cherry tomatoes

4 tbsp / 60ml mild extra-virgin olive oil

½ tsp sugar

6 basil sprigs, leaves torn

Put the mozzarella in a bowl, pour in the cream, and season with salt and pepper. Cover and leave in the fridge for 4 hours.

Sauté the baby tomatoes in a pan with 1 tbsp of the olive oil for about 8 minutes. Add the sugar and a little salt and pepper, shake the pan, and turn the tomatoes over until they soften and some of the skins split.

Serve the mozzarella at room temperature with the tomatoes on the side. Drizzle with the remaining 3 tbsp olive oil and garnish with the torn basil leaves.

SPELT AND TOMATO SALAD

What is new today is often very old, and what was long seen as poor peasant food is now fashionable. This is true of a group of ancient Mediterranean wheat species known as farro (in Italy) and épeautre (in France), similar to our spelt. It's a grain on which the Roman armies are said to have marched. This Tuscan salad is charming and satisfying.

Serves 6

1⅓ cups / 240g spelt or pearled farro
salt
7 oz / 200g baby plum tomatoes, halved
½ red onion, finely chopped
6 tbsp / 90ml extra-virgin olive oil
juice of ½ to 1 lemon, to taste
1 bunch flat-leaf parsley, coarsely chopped
black pepper

Soak the spelt or farro in plenty of cold water for 30 minutes. Rinse, drain, and put it in a pan with plenty of water to cover. Bring to a boil and let simmer for about 20 minutes, or until tender, seasoning with salt toward the end. Drain and put it in a serving bowl.

Add the tomatoes, onion, olive oil, lemon juice, and parsley and season with pepper. Mix well before serving.

Variation

For a simple but delightful Sicilian spelt salad, omit the tomatoes. Instead, mix in 6 tbsp / 50g raisins (soaked in water for 30 minutes), 6 tbsp / 50g lightly toasted pine nuts, and the shredded leaves of three basil sprigs and three mint sprigs.

CAFE DE FRANCE
GEWELT

SHOPPING AT A FARMERS' MARKET IN PROVENCE

Weekly farmers' markets are an important part of the culture and way of life of towns and villages. They are where you meet and socialize and where, visually, the landscape delivers to the table. For me, they are magical.

Going early to choose cheeses and charcuterie, a jam or honey, and olives and then getting something from an artisan cook and eating it sitting on a bench under a plane tree is my idea of happiness. Then coffee or a glass of iced rosé in a café on the square. After a visit to the butcher and fishmonger, stocking up on fruit and vegetables – fleshy red peppers, heirloom tomatoes, zucchini with their blossoms, shiny black eggplants, fat garlic heads. Depending on the season, there might be pumpkins, chestnuts, wild mushrooms in large baskets, peaches and apricots, baskets of figs and Muscat grapes. Finally, going away with a couple of local wines, freshly baked bread, and bunches of herbs, thinking of what I am going to make . . .

POTATO SALAD WITH GREEN OLIVE TAPENADE

A Provençal tapenade aux olives vertes makes a fantastic dressing for potatoes. Use good-quality pitted olives: I use the large Spanish Queen variety. Serve as a first course alone or as part of a sharing menu.

The French peel the potatoes for their salads and the British do not. I peel them before cooking, but you may prefer to boil them in their skins and peel them when cool enough to handle.

Serves 8

2¼ lb / 1kg new potatoes, peeled

4 oz / 115g pitted green olives in brine, drained

7 anchovy fillets in oil, drained

2 tbsp capers, drained

1 to 2 garlic cloves, crushed, to taste

5 tbsp / 75ml extra-virgin olive oil

1½ tbsp wine vinegar or sherry vinegar

salt and black pepper, or Aleppo pepper, to taste

1 bunch flat-leaf parsley, leaves chopped

Cook the potatoes in boiling salted water until tender right through when you pierce them with a knife.

Put the olives, anchovies, capers, garlic, olive oil, and vinegar in a food processor or blender and blend to a thick, rough, oily tapenade. Taste, and adjust the seasoning with salt, black pepper, or Aleppo pepper if needed.

Drain the potatoes and cut them into quarters, or in half if small. Mix with the tapenade until they are well coated and then sprinkle with the parsley leaves before serving.

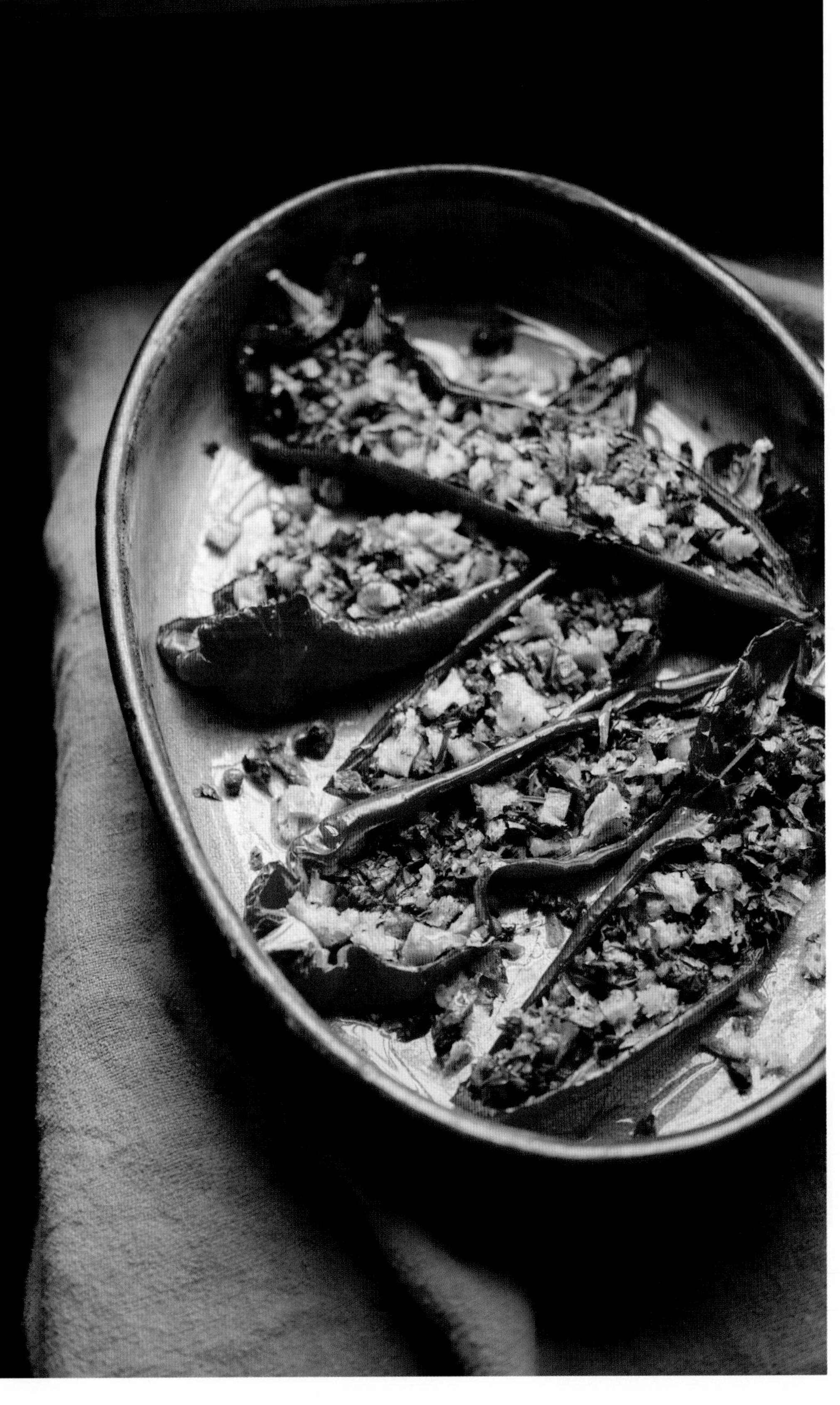

STUFFED PEPPERS WITH BREADCRUMBS, ANCHOVIES, OLIVES, AND CAPERS

I have spent years stuffing vegetables in all kinds of ways – with rice, bulgur, meat, cheese. In my family's culture, laboring over food was a way of expressing love for family and honoring guests, and stuffed vegetables was one of those labor-intensive foods. Now what matters to me is to offer something that delights, and my friends are happier when a dish is quick and easy because they want to make it themselves. These stuffed peppers are quick to make and the stuffing is essentially Mediterranean. Use the long Romano peppers commonly found in Middle Eastern markets, or substitute Anaheim chiles.

Serves 6

3 Romano peppers, slit lengthwise and seeded

6 anchovy fillets in oil, drained and chopped

6 good-quality black olives, such as Kalamata, pitted and chopped

1 tbsp tiny capers in brine, drained

1 small bunch flat-leaf parsley, leaves chopped

scant ¾ cup / 40g fresh breadcrumbs

3 tbsp extra-virgin olive oil

Preheat the oven to 350°F. Line a roasting pan with foil.

Arrange the peppers cut-side up on the foil. Roast for about 30 minutes, until they are soft. Set aside to cool.

Mix together the anchovies, olives, capers, parsley, breadcrumbs, and olive oil to make a stuffing. When the peppers are cool enough to handle, put a little stuffing into each and serve at room temperature.

SPICY ROASTED CARROT SALAD

In Morocco, the appetizers served before a meal are cooked vegetable salads; they often feature carrots, usually flavored with cumin, which is supposed to stimulate the appetite. The mix of spices in this recipe is particularly delicious. I serve the carrots with labneh (see page 45) made with a little salt, flavored with the grated zest of a lemon.

Serves 6 to 8

2¼ lb / 1kg medium carrots, peeled
1½ tsp ground cumin
½ tsp ground coriander
½ tsp ground cinnamon
½ tsp ground ginger
3 garlic cloves, crushed
2 to 3 tbsp olive oil
1 tbsp honey
juice of ½ to 1 lemon, to taste
salt and black pepper
Aleppo pepper, to taste (optional)
2 tbsp extra-virgin olive oil
3 tbsp roughly chopped cilantro

Preheat the oven to 400°F.

Cut the carrots in half crosswise, then cut them in half lengthwise so that you have wide sticks. Put them in a baking dish.

In a bowl, combine the cumin, coriander, cinnamon, ginger, garlic, olive oil, honey, and lemon juice and season with salt and black pepper, and Aleppo pepper (if using). Mix very well and pour over the carrots. Turn them with your hands until they are coated all over.

Bake the carrots for about 1 hour, until tender, turning them over once. Let cool.

Serve at room temperature drizzled with extra-virgin olive oil and sprinkled with the cilantro.

EGGPLANTS WITH POMEGRANATE DRESSING AND YOGURT SAUCE

My grandparents moved to Egypt from Syria when the ancient camel-caravan trade routes from the East through Aleppo became obsolete (because the building of the Suez Canal created a new sea route). They moved into a new quarter that became settled entirely by Syrians. My father, the youngest of eleven and the only boy, was conceived in Syria and born in Cairo. His family always cooked the food of Aleppo. It was part of who we were. This dish, with layers of textures and flavors, is my version of one of the city's delicacies. Serve it as a first course.

Serves 4

olive oil for brushing

2 eggplants (about 10 oz / 285g each), trimmed and cut in half lengthwise

1½ tbsp pomegranate molasses

1½ tbsp red or white wine vinegar

3 tbsp extra-virgin olive oil

salt and black pepper

Yogurt sauce

generous ¾ cup / 200g plain whole-milk yogurt

grated zest of ½ lemon

1 to 2 tbsp tahini, to taste

1 small garlic clove, crushed (optional)

1 tbsp pine nuts

1 tbsp pomegranate seeds

1 tbsp chopped flat-leaf parsley

Preheat the broiler to high. Line a baking sheet with foil, brush it with olive oil, and add the eggplants, cut-side down. Broil for 10 to 15 minutes, until the skins are blistered and the eggplants feel soft inside when you press them – but they should not be too soft. (Alternatively, preheat the oven to 425°F and roast the eggplants for 25 to 30 minutes.)

When the eggplants are cool enough to handle, use a spoon to scoop out the flesh into a colander and let drain for a few minutes.

In a shallow serving dish, cut the eggplant flesh into long strips and then into chunks. Combine the pomegranate molasses, vinegar, and extra-virgin olive oil; season with salt and pepper; beat well with a fork; and pour over the eggplants. Turn the pieces in the dressing to coat them well.

For the yogurt sauce, beat the yogurt with the lemon zest, tahini, and garlic (if using). Spoon it over the eggplants.

Toast the pine nuts in a dry skillet over medium heat for about 3 minutes, shaking the pan until brown spots appear. Keep an eye on them as they will burn quickly. Sprinkle over the dish along with the pomegranate seeds and parsley before serving.

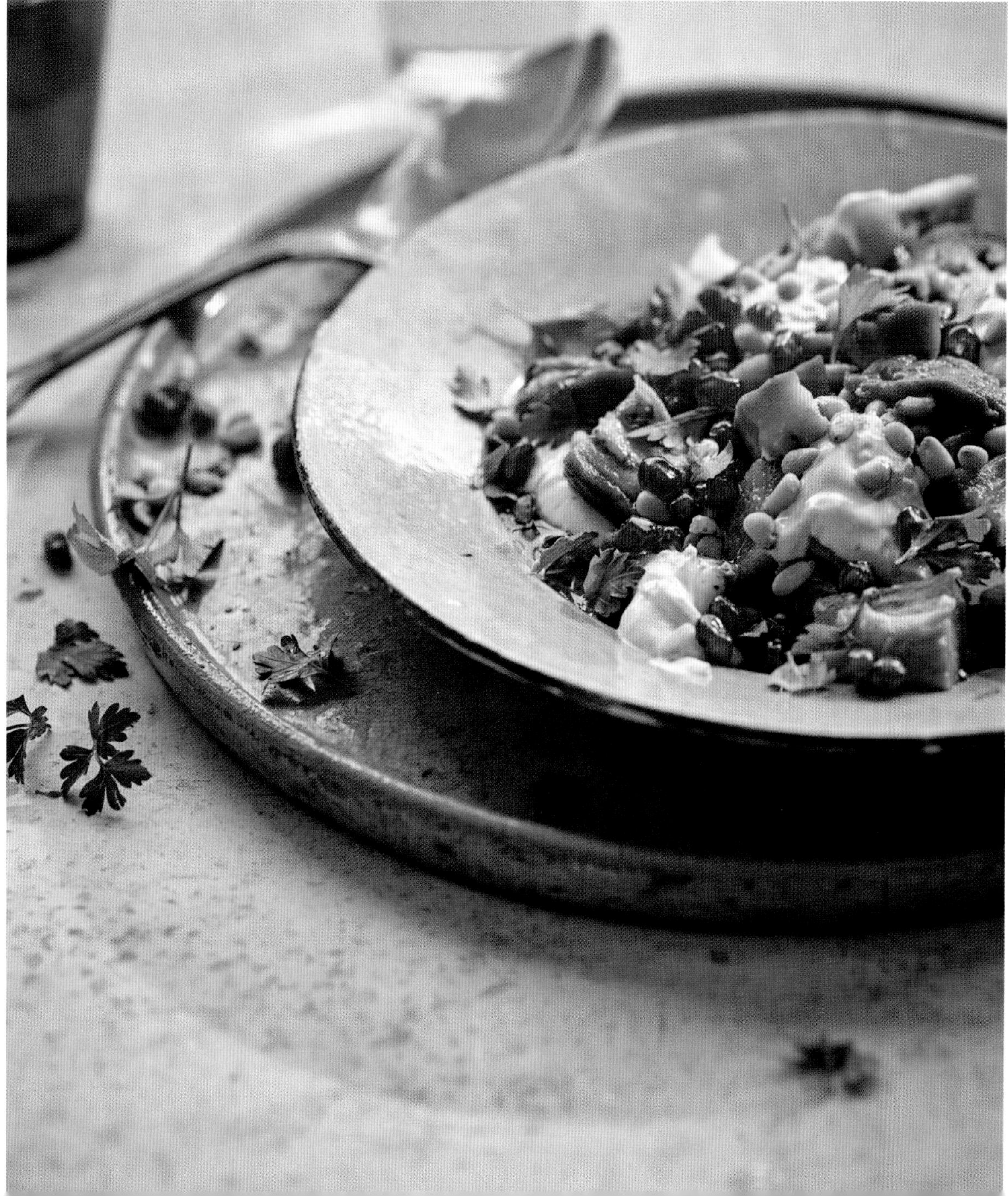

EGGPLANT IN A SPICY HONEY SAUCE WITH SOFT GOAT CHEESE

These are flavors of Morocco that you will encounter in Marseille. Use a delicately scented honey, such as orange blossom or acacia. Make the dish in advance to allow the eggplant to absorb the sauce and then serve at room temperature as a first course or as one of three or four "sharing" dishes. It's wonderful.

Serves 4 to 6

4 tbsp / 60ml olive oil or sunflower oil

2 eggplants, trimmed and cut into ⅜-inch-thick slices

salt

3 garlic cloves, crushed

1 tbsp grated fresh ginger

3 tbsp lemon juice

4 tbsp / 85g honey

1 large pinch Aleppo pepper, or to taste

1 tbsp extra-virgin olive oil

10 oz / 285g fresh soft goat cheese, cut into pieces

1 tbsp chopped flat-leaf parsley

Warm 1½ tbsp of the oil in a nonstick sauté pan with a tight lid over medium-high heat. Add half of the eggplant slices, sprinkle lightly with salt, and cook, covered, for about 15 minutes, turning the eggplant over at least once, until soft and browned all over. (They fry and steam at the same time.) Remove and set aside, then repeat with another 1½ tbsp oil, the remaining eggplant slices, and a sprinkling of salt.

Warm the remaining 1 tbsp oil with the garlic in a small skillet over low heat for moments only, stirring constantly, until the aroma rises and the garlic just begins to color. Remove from the heat and stir in the ginger, lemon juice, honey, Aleppo pepper, extra-virgin olive oil, and a little salt. Mix well and taste to get the balance of sweet and salt just right.

Return all the eggplant slices to the sauté pan and pour in the honey sauce. Cook over low heat for 2 to 3 minutes, turning the slices to coat them in the sauce. If it seems too dry, add 1 to 3 tbsp water.

Arrange the eggplant on a serving dish with the goat cheese on the side and sprinkle with the chopped parsley before serving.

CHICKPEAS WITH YOGURT AND TAHINI SAUCE

Many years ago – during the Lebanese civil war – I received a letter from Beirut, from someone I didn't know. The late Josephine Salam once wrote that she had some recipes for me and offered to come to my house and cook them with me. We made so much food that we had to call my neighbors in to help eat it up. After that, we often cooked together, and as she came and went from Lebanon, I received an ongoing account of everyday life in her ravaged city. She always managed to put humor into the horror. This elegant version of fattet hummus is inspired by her. You can make it with two drained 14-oz / 397g cans chickpeas but it is the kind of dish that is easy to make in large quantities and, in that case, it is worth making with dried chickpeas.

Serves 4 to 6

1 cup / 160g dried chickpeas, soaked overnight in double their volume of water with 1 tsp baking soda

¼ tsp baking soda

salt

1⅔ cups / 400g plain yogurt, at room temperature

2 tbsp tahini

1 to 2 garlic cloves, crushed

7 tbsp / 50g pine nuts

2 tbsp extra-virgin olive oil

1 tbsp pomegranate molasses

1 good pinch Aleppo pepper (optional)

1 tbsp chopped flat-leaf parsley

1 pita bread, cut open and into triangles, very lightly toasted

Drain the chickpeas and put them in a pan with enough water to cover by about ½ inch. Stir in the ¼ tsp baking soda (it helps them to soften). Bring to a boil, skimming off the foam that forms at the top. Simmer, covered, for 20 to 45 minutes, until the chickpeas are soft (the time depends on their type and age). Add water if necessary so that the level remains about ½ inch above the chickpeas throughout cooking. When the chickpeas have begun to soften, season with salt.

Mix the yogurt with the tahini and garlic and season with a little salt.

Toast the pine nuts in a dry skillet over medium heat for seconds only, stirring, until very lightly browned.

Drain the chickpeas, put them in a wide serving dish, and pour the yogurt mixture all over them. Drizzle with the olive oil and pomegranate molasses and, if you like, dust with the Aleppo pepper. Sprinkle with the pine nuts and parsley.

Serve the chickpeas with the toasted pita triangles stuck around the edges.

MASHED CHICKPEAS WITH TURMERIC

Chickpeas with turmeric is peasant food in Tunisia, but it tastes marvelous. With the addition of some Mediterranean pantry specialties, it becomes a glorious, multicolored party dish.

Serves 6 to 8

1⅔ cups / 300g dried chickpeas, soaked overnight in double their volume of water with 1 tsp baking soda

½ tsp baking soda

5 garlic cloves, peeled

¾ to 1 tsp ground turmeric, to taste

6 tbsp / 90ml extra-virgin olive oil

juice of 1 lemon

salt and black pepper

Optional additions

16 black olives, such as Kalamata

3 to 4 piquillo peppers in oil, drained and halved

1 boiled lemon (see page 226) or preserved lemon, cut into small pieces

1 tbsp drained capers

3 tbsp chopped cilantro leaves

Drain the chickpeas and put them in a large pan with enough water to cover by about ½ inch. Stir in the ½ tsp baking soda (it helps them to soften). Bring to a boil, skimming off the foam that forms at the top, and then add the garlic and stir in the turmeric. Simmer, covered, for 20 to 45 minutes, until the chickpeas are very tender (the time depends on their type and age). Add water if necessary to keep them covered. By the end of cooking, the liquid should be reduced to a thick sauce. If not, remove the lid and cook, uncovered, to reduce it.

Set aside a small handful of chickpeas to use as garnish. Add the olive oil and lemon juice to the pan, season with salt and pepper, and blend to a rough paste, using an immersion blender or food processor.

Spread the paste, hot or cold, in a wide shallow serving platter and garnish with the reserved chickpeas, plus, if you like, one or more of the optional additions.

SPICY BULGUR AND NUT SALAD

This is a Syrian dish, and my family called it *bazargan* because all the ingredients could be bought at the spice bazaar in Aleppo. It is substantial and filling and also amazingly rich and tasty, with a variety of nuts, spices, and aromatics. It is easy to make for a lot of people, can be prepared in advance, and keeps perfectly well for days. There is also no cooking because bulgur is wheat that has been boiled, dried, and then "cracked" – it only needs soaking in boiling water, while all the aromatic ingredients are beaten together as a dressing.

Serve as a first course with Greek yogurt or labneh (see page 45). It can be served in a large bowl or elegantly rolled into balls the size of a walnut and cupped in Little Gem lettuce leaves.

Serves 6

1½ cups / 250g bulgur

1⅔ cups / 395ml lightly salted boiling water

7 tbsp / 100ml mild extra-virgin olive oil

1½ tbsp pomegranate molasses

salt

juice of 2½ lemons

¼ cup / 65g tomato paste

1 to 1½ tbsp harissa or other hot pepper paste, to taste

1½ tsp ground cumin

1 tsp ground coriander

½ tsp ground allspice

1 cup / 100g walnuts, lightly toasted

¾ cup / 100g hazelnuts, lightly toasted

5 tbsp / 50g pistachios, lightly toasted

7 tbsp / 50g pine nuts, lightly toasted

1 large bunch flat-leaf parsley, leaves chopped

pomegranate seeds for garnish (optional)

Put the bulgur in a large bowl and pour the boiling water over it. Let soak for 30 minutes, until the grains are very tender. Stir occasionally so that the water is absorbed evenly.

Combine the olive oil with the pomegranate molasses and season with salt. Add the lemon juice, tomato paste, harissa, cumin, coriander, and allspice and beat vigorously with a fork until well blended. Pour over the bulgur and mix very well. Taste and add more salt if necessary.

Coarsely chop the walnuts, hazelnuts, and pistachios. Add them to the bulgur, stir in the pine nuts and parsley; mix well. If you like, garnish with pomegranate seeds before serving.

YOGURT AND CUCUMBER SALAD

In this deconstruction of a famous Middle Eastern classic known more widely by its Greek name *tzatziki*, grated cucumber, cloaked in a minty dressing with a touch of orange blossom water, is a topping on creamy yogurt flavored with garlic and lemon zest. It is a perfect side to so many dishes in this book – except fish. In Turkey, it is taboo to serve yogurt with fish, so I don't.

Serves 4

3 small cucumbers, or 1 large one

salt

3 tbsp extra-virgin olive oil

1 tsp orange blossom water

2 tbsp lemon juice, plus grated zest of 1 lemon

1 mint sprig, leaves finely chopped

generous ¾ cup / 200g Greek yogurt

1 or 2 garlic cloves, crushed

Peel and grate the cucumbers and put in a colander. Sprinkle very generously with salt and mix well, using your hands. Let drain for 30 minutes.

In a medium bowl, whisk together the olive oil, orange blossom water, lemon juice, and mint and pour over the cucumber.

In another bowl, beat together the yogurt, lemon zest, and garlic. Add a little salt if you like (I don't) and spread on a serving plate. Just before serving, top with the cucumber.

MEDITERRANEAN PANTRY SALAD

This is a snack for when people visit unexpectedly and stay on. I make it as we sit in the kitchen with a drink. It is inspired by a bar in Barcelona that displayed a huge array of jars and cans and specialized in tapas made entirely from preserves. I've added fresh tomatoes and hard-boiled eggs and serve it with good bread.

Serves 4

4 red piquillo peppers in oil, drained

one 7-oz / 200g can tuna, drained

one 2-oz / 55g can anchovies, drained

12 black olives

4 ripe plum tomatoes, cut into wedges

4 hard-boiled eggs, quartered lengthwise

3 tbsp extra-virgin olive oil

1 tbsp white wine vinegar

salt and black pepper

Divide the piquillos, tuna, anchovies, olives, tomatoes, and eggs among four plates. In a medium bowl, beat together the olive oil and vinegar, season with salt and black pepper, and then drizzle over each helping.

VEGETABLE SIDES AND SHARING DISHES

Vegetables have an important place in this part of the world where – until relatively recently – much of the population consisted of impoverished peasants who could rarely afford meat; in some countries, maybe only once a week and sometimes only on festive occasions.

The Vaucluse is a department of Provence where I often stayed with my friend, the late Dutch sculptor Ans Hey, and which is incredibly appealing. Everything is radiant: the luminous sky, its colors fading into pastel tints in the dazzling light; the earth gray and ocher; the houses white or rose or rusty gold; the luxurious vegetation pale, not vivid green. Against it, the different reds of the winter roses and the geraniums and bougainvilleas that come out in the spring are electrifying. The smells are of fig trees or Aleppo pines, or orange and lemon blossom and jasmine and a whole variety of wild herbs basking in the sun. But when I asked farmers how they were, they always replied, "C'est la catastrophe!" Either the south wind blew just before harvest time and the crops dried out, or they were attacked by frost, or the rains carried away the seed. The reality behind the charm for those living off the land can be one of hardship and constant struggle, where everything is gained by painful effort.

Everywhere in the Mediterranean it is dry with hot summers and mild winters, with rare but violent rainstorms and strong winds. The soil is generally poor and often stony and shallow, and only a small part can be cultivated. Crops are at the mercy of the unstable elements. Lands under cultivation are scattered between great stretches of scrub and forest, both on plains and on mountain slopes, and in parts where the desert allows. The olive and the vine are classic types of Mediterranean vegetation that require little moisture. Their long roots, which seek out water deep in the soil, also help them resist the wind's attack. In the past, wheat, corn, and barley were important cereal crops that were sometimes rotated with chickpeas, lentils, and fava beans.

But the grain fields have receded to make way for fruit groves and market gardens and for single-crop cultivation. Although some of the Mediterranean has remained attached to the idea of smallholders growing a variety of crops for the local market, the trend has been for specialized, mass-produced cultivation directed toward the export market.

In an impoverished rural world where the morrow is uncertain, you have to be careful and frugal. Part of the charm of Mediterranean cooking is its sobriety. It is the combination of frugality and fruitfulness, with an abundance of vegetables, grain, pulses, fruit, and nuts, that gives it a unique, rustic, healthy quality. Every country has the same vegetables but each has its favorites and each has its special ways of making them a pleasure to eat. When I asked an Italian chef what made the food of the south special, he said a little "fantasia." He meant the little personal touches that give real flavor. Around the Mediterranean, these can be the addition of just one herb or a trickle of olive oil to a hot, spicy, peppery sauce.

VEGETABLES POACHED IN STOCK AND WHITE WINE

A usual way to cook vegetables in the Mediterranean is to lightly poach in water and then serve with a little salt and a drizzle of extra-virgin olive oil. It is what I cook for myself every day.

For their versions of the vegetable side dish, the nouvelle cuisine chefs of Provence brought tiny baby vegetables into fashion. The chefs poached the vegetables briefly in stock, sometimes with a little white wine added, and served them with garden-fresh herbs. I adopted this method, and when I have many people for dinner I often serve a large platter with a collection of pretty little vegetables as a first course or side dish. I arrange them pell-mell and dress them with a mild-tasting extra-virgin olive oil and a sprinkling of fresh herbs. Everyone loves it.

You can make this in advance and warm it in the oven covered in foil, or serve at room temperature.

Half-fill a large pan with chicken or vegetable stock or white wine. Bring to a boil and add salt, three or four peeled garlic cloves, four bay leaves, and two thyme sprigs. Keeping the stock or white wine at a low simmer, add your choice of vegetables in the order in which they need to cook until only just tender. Baby carrots and tiny new potatoes may need about 10 minutes, asparagus 2 to 3 minutes. Try two, three, or four vegetables: baby carrots, tiny new potatoes, baby leeks and artichoke hearts, fava beans, green beans, baby zucchini, cauliflower florets, peas, asparagus spears, and Little Gem lettuces cut in half.

SPRING VEGETABLE MEDLEY

I found this trio of spring vegetables – fava beans, peas, and artichokes – cooked together in several countries. I've adopted an Italian version in which they are cooked in a light broth (called *vignole* in Tuscany, *vignarola* in Rome, and *frittedda* in Sicily). I make it throughout the year with artichoke hearts in jars and frozen fava beans and petite peas. I eat it with a spoon, like a soup, and have even served it over pasta as pasta primavera. If you have some dry white wine on hand, put some in with the broth. In Spain, they add 1 to 2 tbsp of brandy. When I use fresh vegetables in spring, I replace the artichokes with asparagus spears.

Serves 4 to 6

2 tbsp olive oil

1 onion, chopped

2 cups / 250g frozen fava beans, thawed

4 baby artichoke hearts in oil, rinsed, halved, and grilled

2 cups / 480ml chicken or vegetable stock, or ¾ cup / 175ml dry white wine and 1¼ cups / 300ml stock

generous ¾ cup / 250g frozen petite peas, thawed

salt and black pepper

1 tsp sugar (optional)

1 mint sprig, leaves torn

1½ tbsp extra-virgin olive oil

Warm the olive oil in a sauté pan over medium-low heat and fry the onion, stirring often, for about 8 minutes, until soft. Add the fava beans, artichokes, and stock or wine and stock. Stir well and simmer, covered, for 15 minutes.

Stir the peas into the pan and cook, covered, for 5 minutes, until all the vegetables are tender. Taste and season with salt and pepper; if you have used dry white wine, you might need to add the sugar. Stir in the mint and serve drizzled with the extra-virgin olive oil.

ROAST SUMMER VEGETABLES

In Provence, ratatouille is a matter of heated debate – do you fry the vegetables separately, one at a time, or sauté them in the same pan, adding them at different times? Roasting the vegetables is much easier and it intensifies their flavors. Serve as a side dish or first course, accompanied by slices of toasted bread brushed with extra-virgin olive oil. Alternatively, serve hot on a bed of creamy polenta (see page 146) or with pasta. The sweet-and-sour variation below makes a good cold appetizer.

Serves 6 to 8

2 eggplants, trimmed and cut into 1¼-inch chunks

2 zucchini, trimmed and cut into 1¼-inch slices

2 red onions, each cut into 6 wedges

8 small tomatoes

3 thyme or marjoram sprigs, leaves only

6 tbsp / 90ml olive oil

salt and black pepper

2 red bell peppers, seeded and cut into 1¼-inch pieces

2 whole heads of garlic, cloves peeled

Position two racks in the upper and lower thirds of the oven and preheat to 350°F. Line two large sheet pans with foil.

Put the eggplants, zucchini, onions, and tomatoes on the pans and sprinkle with the thyme or marjoram, olive oil, salt, and black pepper. Mix well, turning the vegetables over so that they are coated in the oil. Place a sheet pan on each oven rack and bake for 30 minutes, then take the pans out of the oven.

Turn over the vegetables in the pan that was on the lower oven rack, add the bell peppers, and put the pan back in the oven on the higher rack. Turn over the vegetables in the other pan, add the garlic, and put it on the lower rack. Roast both pans for 15 to 20 minutes longer, until the vegetables are very soft. If they become brown before they are tender, cover them with foil. Serve hot or at room temperature.

Variations

~ Garnish with one or two of the following: lightly toasted sliced almonds or pine nuts, chopped flat-leaf parsley, garlic croutons, feta cheese cut into cubes.

~ For a sweet-and-sour version to serve cold: heat 6 tbsp / 90ml white or red wine vinegar with 3 tbsp sugar and stir to dissolve the sugar; sprinkle over the hot vegetables, toss well, and let cool.

HERBY MASHED POTATOES WITH OLIVE OIL

You will be won over by this Mediterranean counterpart to the mashed potatoes with butter, milk, and cream that we all love. It makes a wonderful side to many dishes in this book, both hot and cold. I can happily eat it by itself.

Serves 6

1 lb 10 oz / 750g Yukon gold potatoes, peeled

6 tbsp / 90ml extra-virgin olive oil, or a half-and-half mix of olive oil and sunflower oil

salt and black pepper

1 handful chopped flat-leaf parsley

3 green onions, finely chopped (optional)

Boil the potatoes in salted water until soft. Drain, keeping about ⅔ cup / 160ml of the cooking water.

Mash the potatoes roughly with a potato masher or a fork and beat in the oil. Season with salt and pepper and stir in a little of the cooking water – enough to give a soft, slightly moist texture. Stir in the parsley and, if you like, the green onions before serving.

Variation

Instead of parsley, mix in another chopped fresh herb, such as basil, mint, dill, or chives.

LEMONY ROAST POTATOES WITH CHERRY TOMATOES AND GARLIC

I love potatoes with lemon. Sweet roasted cherry tomatoes and soft, mildly bitter garlic add complexity to a dish that is delightful hot or cold.

Serves 6

2¼ lb / 1kg waxy new potatoes

5 to 6 tbsp / 75 to 90ml olive oil or sunflower oil

juice of 1½ lemons

salt and black pepper

10 oz / 285g cherry tomatoes

6 garlic cloves, peeled and cut in half lengthwise (optional)

1 large handful cilantro or dill, coarsely chopped

Cook the potatoes, in their skins, in boiling water for about 10 minutes, then drain. Cut into slices about ½ inch thick, then put them in a wide baking dish.

Meanwhile, preheat the oven to 475°F.

Combine the oil and lemon juice, season with salt and pepper, and beat with a fork. Pour over the potatoes and use your hands to turn the slices until they are well coated. Add the tomatoes and the garlic (if using).

Roast the potatoes for 20 to 30 minutes, turning them once, until crisp and brown. Serve sprinkled with the cilantro or dill.

Sicilia
Kilo
€3.50

ROAST CELERY ROOT, SWEET POTATO, AND CARROT WITH TARRAGON VINAIGRETTE

The sweet anise and slightly vanilla flavor of tarragon in the dressing adds an intriguing note to this root vegetable bake. It is a perfect winter accompaniment to meat and poultry grills and roasts and can also be eaten cold as a salad.

Serves 6

1 celery root

3 sweet potatoes

3 carrots

salt and black pepper

3 tbsp olive oil or sunflower oil

Tarragon vinaigrette

3 tbsp extra-virgin olive oil

1 tbsp vinegar

salt and black pepper

5 tarragon sprigs, leaves stripped and coarsely chopped

Preheat the oven to 400°F. Line a large roasting pan with foil.

Peel the celery root, sweet potatoes, and carrots and cut them into chunks of about 1¼ inches. Put them in the roasting pan, sprinkle with salt and pepper, and pour the oil over them. Use your hands to turn the vegetables until they are well coated.

Roast the vegetables for 50 to 60 minutes, turning them once, until tender and lightly browned in places. Cover with foil if they are getting too brown toward the end of the cooking time.

For the vinaigrette, combine the extra-virgin olive oil and vinegar, season with salt and pepper, beat with a fork, then stir in the tarragon.

Pour the vinaigrette over the roasted vegetables, turning them so that they are well coated, and then serve.

FRITTATA WITH CHEESE AND HERBS

This is a Slovenian frtalja. When I was a child, my nanny, Maria Koron, was a Slovene from a village called Batuje in a part of Slovenia that had been taken by Italy during the First World War. She talked to us in Italian and cooked for us when we were small. A few years ago, I was contacted by Barbara Skubic, who was part of an organization of women who were finding out about their mothers' and grandmothers' lives in Egypt. They found me through a cake called *potica*, which Maria made, that appeared in one of my books. In her first letter, Barbara had a list of questions about Maria. The last one was "Did you love her?" I replied "We adored her!" I was invited to take part in a festival of Egypt in Ljubljana. I got to meet Maria's family and to visit her village. I learned that she had been a novice nun, something she never told us, but was convinced by her family to go to work in Egypt and send money home, as was usual in Slovenia at the time. I brought back to London her family's own salamis, cheeses, wines, and potica.

I vary the herbs, depending on what I have on hand, from parsley or tarragon alone to a mix of two or three, such as chives, dill, basil, mint. Use scissors to snip chives into small pieces, or basil leaves into larger ones.

Accompanied by sour cream or yogurt and a salad, this makes a light meal.

Serves 2

4½ tbsp / 40g all-purpose flour
7 tbsp / 100ml whole milk
4 eggs
3½ oz / 100g mature Cheddar, grated
½ tsp salt
¼ tsp black pepper
½ cup / 20g snipped fresh herbs
1½ tbsp butter

Put the flour in a bowl and gradually add the milk, beating vigorously with a fork, then beat in the eggs to make a batter.

Stir in the cheese, salt, pepper, and herbs – there should be plenty of herbs and the frittata should be quite green.

Warm the butter in a small nonstick skillet over medium-low heat. Swirl it around until it sizzles, then pour in the batter and cook for about 8 minutes, until the bottom and sides are set.

Meanwhile, preheat the broiler to hot.

Put the skillet under the broiler for about 1 minute to set the top. It should still be creamy. Serve hot.

POTATO OMELET

This comforting omelet should be *really* creamy inside. For an Italian frittata di patate alle erbe, serve with the herb dressing. For a Tunisian version, serve with the spicy tomato "jam."

Serves 4 to 6

10 oz / 285g potatoes, peeled and cut into similar-size pieces

4 tbsp / 60ml olive oil

2 onions, halved and sliced

6 eggs

salt and black pepper

Boil the potatoes for about 15 minutes, until tender, then drain and mash them roughly.

Warm 2 tbsp of the olive oil in a nonstick skillet over low heat and fry the onions for about 15 minutes, stirring often, until soft, then turn up the heat to medium-high and stir constantly until golden. Remove from the heat.

Beat the eggs with a fork. When the potatoes and onions have cooled a little, add them to the eggs and mix well. Season with salt and pepper.

Preheat the broiler to very hot. Wipe out the skillet with paper towels and warm the remaining 2 tbsp olive oil over medium-low heat. Pour in the egg-onion-potato mixture and cook for 3 to 4 minutes, until the bottom is set and lightly browned, shaking the pan to make sure that the omelet does not stick. Then put it under the broiler for about 2 minutes, until the top is dry and slightly springy to the touch. The omelet should be creamy – it is fine if it is still a little liquid inside.

Serve warm or at room temperature.

Variations

~ For an Italian herb dressing: mix 2 tbsp lemon juice with 6 tbsp / 90ml extra-virgin olive oil, 2 tbsp chopped fresh tarragon, 1 tsp grated orange zest, and some salt and black pepper.

~ For a Tunisian tomato "jam": put 1½ cups / 400g canned diced tomatoes in a skillet and stir in 1 tbsp honey and 1 tbsp rose water. Cook over medium heat for 10 minutes, until thick and jammy. Season with a little salt and plenty of Aleppo pepper and cook for 2 minutes more.

BEATTIE

TARTE PISSALADIÈRE

I find the combination of anchovy fillets and meltingly soft onions irresistible. The pissaladière is at the heart of the cuisine of Nice, but in Nice they tell you it was born in neighboring Liguria. I was in Nice with Alan Davidson when we were booked to entertain the wives at an international frozen-food conference with stories about food. In the end we entertained the husbands, too. Mary Bloom, an American journalist at the *International Herald Tribune* who was writing a humor piece about the event, invited us to dinner at the great Jacques Maximin's Chantecler at the Negresco. It was a fantastic Mediterranean menu dégustation by one of the first innovative chefs, and the pissaladière was on a shortcrust base instead of the usual yeast dough.

Serves 6

Shortcrust pastry

9 tbsp / 125g unsalted butter
1¾ cups / 250g all-purpose flour
¼ tsp salt
1 egg, separated
1 to 2 tbsp milk, if necessary

Filling

¼ cup / 60ml olive oil
4 large onions, halved and sliced
¾ tsp salt
½ tsp black pepper
16 anchovy fillets in oil, drained
6 pitted black olives, halved

For the pastry, cut the butter into small pieces and rub it into the flour and salt until the texture is like damp sand. Add the egg yolk, mix well, and work very briefly with your hand until the dough holds together in a soft ball, adding a little of the milk if necessary. Wrap in plastic wrap or wax paper and let rest in a cool place for 1 hour.

For the filling, warm the olive oil in a large sauté pan with a lid over very low heat. Add the onions and cook, covered, stirring often, for 55 to 60 minutes, until they are meltingly soft, almost a purée but not at all colored (if they start to turn brown before they are soft, add 2 to 3 tbsp water). Add the salt and pepper and cook, uncovered, to let any liquid evaporate.

Preheat the oven to 400°F. Grease a 10-inch shallow tart pan with a removable bottom. Line the pan with the pastry, pressing it firmly up the sides with the palm of your hand (with this soft dough, it's easier than rolling). Prick the bottom of the pastry with a fork and brush with the egg white. Bake for 10 minutes.

Spread the onions over the crust, arrange the anchovy fillets in a lattice pattern on top, and press the olives into the onions in between the lattice. Bake for about 20 minutes.

Serve hot or warm, cut into wedges.

POTATOES, ASPARAGUS TIPS, AND EGGS

My daughter Anna and her three daughters, Sarah, Ruby, and Nelly, asked for recipes for the dishes I have cooked for them since I started this book. They became passionate cooks and my most important testers, with Anna making meticulous notes and suggestions. This simple bake has become one of their regular snack meals.

Serves 4

1 lb / 450g new potatoes, peeled
7 oz / 200g asparagus tips
salt and black pepper
4 to 5 tbsp / 60 to 75ml olive oil
2 tbsp butter
4 eggs

Cook the potatoes in boiling water until they are tender.

Meanwhile, preheat the oven to 400°F.

Slice the cooked potatoes into a baking dish. Add the asparagus tips, sprinkle with salt and a little pepper, and drizzle with the olive oil. Turn the vegetables until they are evenly coated.

Bake the asparagus until tender, 15 to 20 minutes depending on how thick the asparagus tips are.

In a large skillet over medium heat, melt the butter and fry the eggs, then sprinkle with salt. The yolks should be still runny.

Serve the eggs on top of the vegetables.

WITH GRAIN

The entire Mediterranean region depends on agriculture. The soil and the climate are ideal for growing old-world vegetables and grain, as well as those from the Americas. Wheat was part of the famous triad, with grapes and olives, that the Greeks and Romans planted throughout the ancient world, and is eaten today as pasta, bulgur, and couscous. Barley is indigenous to the region, rice was introduced by the Arabs, and corn came from the Americas.

At an empty café in the Piazza del Campo in Siena, an old man sat alone at the next table. I smiled. Pointing to a chair, he said, "Join me." Telling him I was researching the local food and inquiring if I could ask him about it, I took out my pad and started, "What region are you from? What did your parents and grandparents do? What are your favorite dishes?" He did not expect that but was happy to chat. He told me his name was Giuseppe and his was a family of ten. They had been peasant farmers on an estate in Tuscany. They had cultivated the land and given half the produce to the landlord as rent. They had grown wheat, vegetables, and fruit; had olive trees; kept pigs, rabbits, and hens; and made wine, olive oil, and salami. They ate what they grew – tomatoes, pumpkins, artichokes, spinach, zucchini, other things, too – and pasta. There was an herb, usually sage or rosemary. The family no longer farmed. Giuseppe was helping to organize the Palio, the horse race between the city contrade (neighborhoods). His favorite dish was chicken with grapes.

In Italy, in the 1980s, I was hearing so many similar stories. Country life had changed dramatically in the 1960s when the system of sharecropping was abolished. People left the land to work in factories, and landowners sold their estates to entrepreneurs who started intensive farming with tractors and machinery.

The old agriculture of intermingled vines, mulberry, and olive trees on the hill slopes, with little patches of wheat, corn, and pulses, where large families of tenants had spent their days fighting their way through the entanglements to pick everything by hand, was replaced by a single-crop industrial agriculture.

But the dishes that were born in the old life never disappeared and are now very popular. Every generation has a way of pulling out from tradition what fits their ideology and what they love. We, too, love rustic food. On a weeklong gastronomic visit to Puglia with a group of American chefs and food writers, we were sometimes given a choice of menu by the hosts. The group always said they wanted cucina povera (poor food), which was trending in America. We were given the local national dish of fave e cicoria, a purée of cooked mashed dried fava beans with bitter leaves that was sometimes served as a soup and sometimes as a pasta.

Dishes that combine grain and vegetables are ideal vegetarian fare, substantial enough to serve as a main dish, easy to partner with other dishes, and also perfect, in a small portion, as a first course before meat or fish. They are born of the land and linked to an old rural way of life. That is why they have powerful nostalgic appeal.

VEGETABLE COUSCOUS

This looks complex, with lots of ingredients, but is really easy. I make it when I have invited a lot of people and I know some of them are vegetarian. Instead of cooking the vegetables in the broth, I roast them so they keep their individual flavors, and I enrich the broth with herbs and spices. I prepare it all in advance – the grain in a huge terra-cotta dish that can go from the oven to the table – preheat the oven to 350°F. Cover the dish of couscous with foil and put it in the oven, and put the vegetables on the rack underneath for 15 minutes. I usually also serve the tomato "jam" from page 155 alongside.

Serves 8

3 eggplants, trimmed and cut into 1½-inch chunks

2 red bell peppers, seeded and cut into 1½-inch pieces

14 oz / 400g butternut squash, seeded and cut into slices or cubes

1 celery root, peeled and cut into 1¼-inch chunks

2 carrots, peeled and cut into 1¼-inch slices

salt

½ cup / 120ml olive oil

3 cups / 480g couscous

Broth

2 tbsp olive oil

1 large onion, chopped

3 garlic cloves, chopped

1 large tomato, peeled and chopped

5 cups / 1.2L vegetable stock

1 cinnamon stick

¼ tsp ground allspice

½ tsp ground ginger

1 good pinch saffron threads, or 1 tsp ground turmeric

One 14-oz / 397g can chickpeas, drained and rinsed (optional)

salt and black pepper

1 large bunch cilantro, leaves chopped

1 bunch flat-leaf parsley, leaves chopped

1 to 2 tbsp harissa, or to taste

Preheat the oven to 350°F. Arrange all the vegetables in one or two foil-lined roasting pans, sprinkle with salt and drizzle 6 tbsp / 90ml of the olive oil over them, tossing to coat them all over. Roast the vegetables for 45 minutes, or until very soft, turning them over once.

Put the couscous into a large baking dish you can serve it in. Add about 1 tsp salt to 3 cups / 720ml warm water and gradually pour this all over the couscous, stirring to absorb evenly. Let swell for 10 minutes, stirring a couple of times. Now, here is the secret for fluffy couscous; stir in the remaining 2 tbsp olive oil and rub the couscous between your hands above the dish to aerate the grains and break up any lumps.

For the broth, warm the olive oil in a stockpot over low heat and fry the onion, stirring, until soft. Add the garlic and stir for a few seconds, until the aroma rises, then add the tomato and cook, stirring, for 3 minutes. Pour in the stock and add the cinnamon stick, allspice, ginger, saffron or turmeric, and chickpeas (if using). Bring to a boil, season with salt and pepper, then simmer over low heat for 10 minutes. Bring the broth to a boil, take off the heat, and stir in the chopped cilantro and parsley.

Put two ladlefuls of the hot broth in a bowl or pitcher and mix in the harissa.

Fluff up the steaming-hot couscous with a fork, breaking up any lumps. Ladle some of the broth over the couscous, enough to moisten but not so much that it is swimming in broth. Pass the rest on the side for guests to help themselves to more as they wish. Serve the couscous in bowls or soup plates with the vegetables on top, and pass the peppery harissa sauce for everyone to help themselves.

CREAMY POLENTA WITH MUSHROOMS

One magical night on the terrace overlooking the canal at the Gritti Palace in Venice, I attended a banquet for chefs from around Italy. The menu represented traditional dishes from all the regions. The local offering was wild mushrooms on creamy polenta. The wild mushrooms were magnificent – I had seen basketfuls at the Rialto market earlier, and the polenta was ever so light and creamy. Shiitake and cremini mushrooms are also lovely cooked this way.

Serves 4

1 lb 1 oz / 740g mushrooms

¼ cup / 60ml extra-virgin olive oil

2 garlic cloves, peeled

salt and black pepper

3 tbsp dry white wine (if you have an open bottle)

7 tbsp / 100ml chicken or vegetable stock

2 tbsp chopped flat-leaf parsley

Creamy polenta

4 cups / 950ml whole milk or water

½ tsp salt

1⅓ cups / 165g instant polenta

4 tsp butter

1¾ oz / 50g Parmesan or Grana Padano, grated

Clean off any dirt from the mushrooms and trim the ends of the stems if necessary. Leave them whole or cut large ones in half.

Warm the olive oil and garlic in a large sauté pan over high heat. Add the mushrooms and cook quickly for 2 minutes, turning them over with a spatula and seasoning with salt and pepper. The mushrooms will absorb the oil and release their liquid. When it evaporates, add the wine (if using) and stock and cook over medium heat for about 4 minutes, until the liquid is reduced a little. Remove the garlic and stir in the parsley.

For the polenta, pour the milk or water into a large pan, add the salt, and bring to a boil. Take the pan off the heat and pour in the polenta in a thin stream, whisking vigorously, then continue to cook over low heat, stirring continuously with the whisk or a wooden spoon for 2 minutes to avoid lumps forming. Cover the pan and cook over very low heat for another 8 minutes. It will gurgle and splatter. Then stir in the butter and the cheese.

Serve the polenta with the mushrooms on top.

Variations

~ For a stronger mushroom flavor, pour 1 cup / 240ml boiling water over 1½ oz / 40g dried porcini and let soak for 30 minutes. Pour off most of the soaking water – leaving behind any grit – and use instead of the stock. Add the drained porcini to the fresh mushrooms.

~ If you want to make the polenta in advance, pour it into a well-oiled baking dish to a thickness of about ¾ inch; reheat in a 400°F oven.

~ For broiled polenta, make the polenta in advance and pour into a well-oiled baking dish to a thickness of about ¾ inch. Let it cool and then cut into four slices. Brush them lightly with olive oil and toast under the broiler until lightly browned on both sides.

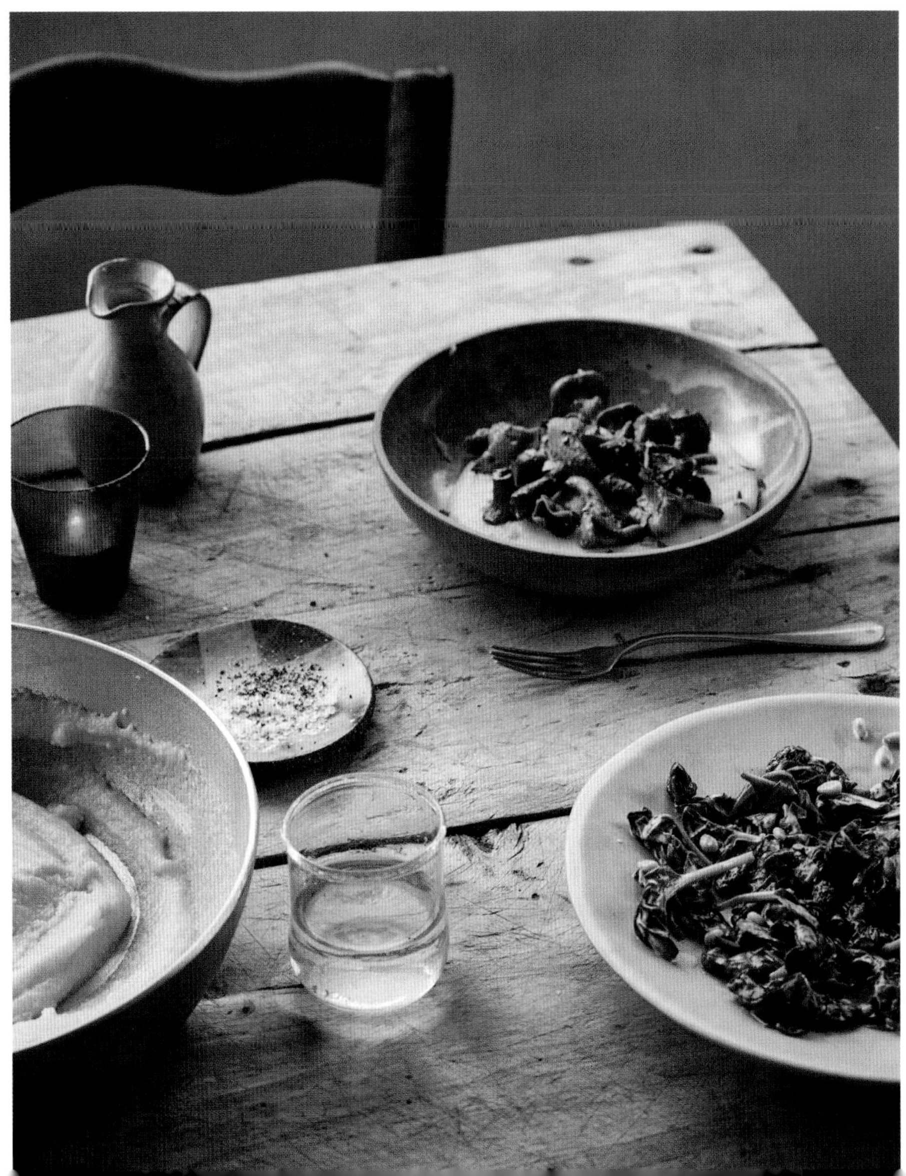

SPINACH, RAISINS, PINE NUTS, AND CRÈME FRAÎCHE WITH POLENTA

I have eaten many lovely spinach dishes, but the Catalan one with raisins and pine nuts is my favorite. The added crème fraîche is my Provençal touch. I serve it on polenta or green tagliatelle.

Serves 4

11 oz / 320g spinach

⅔ cup / 160ml crème fraîche

salt and black pepper

2 tbsp pine nuts, lightly toasted

2 tbsp raisins, soaked in water for 20 minutes

1 recipe Creamy Polenta (see page 146) or broiled polenta (see page 147)

Wash the spinach and, if necessary, remove any thick, tough stems. Drain well. Press the leaves into a big pan. Put the lid on tightly and cook over medium-high heat for moments only, until the leaves crumple into a soft mass. They will steam in the water that clings to them. If the spinach is young and prewashed, put 3 to 4 tbsp water in the pan with the leaves to create the steam.

Pour out any liquid, stir in the crème fraîche, season with salt and pepper, and add the pine nuts and raisins. Stir gently and heat through.

Serve the spinach on the polenta.

Pictured at bottom right on page 147.

BARLEY WITH MUSHROOMS AND CHESTNUTS

This is a heartwarming rural winter dish with a grand finishing touch. You can use hulled barley instead of pearl barley; hulled barley is more nutritious but takes longer to cook and does not result in a creamy dish. The instructions on my supermarket package of pearl barley say it takes 45 to 60 minutes; but if you soak it overnight, the cooking time is shortened to about 30 minutes. Check the package instructions for soaking and cooking the grain.

Serves 4

generous ¾ cup / 165g pearl barley, soaked in plenty of water overnight

3¼ cups / 770ml water

2 chicken or vegetable bouillon cubes

salt

3 tbsp sunflower oil or olive oil

14 oz / 400g cremini mushrooms, quartered

2 garlic cloves, crushed

black pepper

one 6.5-oz / 184g package cooked whole chestnuts

2 to 3 tbsp ruby port

2 tbsp butter, cut into pieces

3 tbsp heavy cream

2 tbsp chopped flat-leaf parsley (optional)

Drain the barley and put it in a pan with the 3¼ cups / 770ml water and bouillon cubes. Season with salt, bring to a boil, cover, and simmer over low heat until tender. Keep checking until the grain is as soft and chewy as you like it. It should be moist with a little liquid. (Add a little water if it gets too dry and drain it if there is too much liquid. If you let it sit, the grain will absorb any remaining liquid and become softer.)

Meanwhile, warm the oil in a large skillet with a lid over high heat. Sauté the mushrooms, covered, turning them over once and shaking the pan, until they release their juices. Remove the lid and let the juices evaporate, then add the garlic, season with salt and pepper, and cook, stirring, for a minute or two. Add the chestnuts and port and cook for 2 minutes more.

You can do all this in advance. Just before you are ready to serve, reheat the barley, adding a little water if necessary, and the mushroom and chestnut mixture. Mix them together, then stir in the butter and cream. Serve sprinkled with the parsley, if you like.

Note

There are some who would serve this with grated Parmesan, but for me it is so good as it is.

GREEN BARLEY "RISOTTO" WITH PEAS AND ASPARAGUS

Although this is called "risotto," it is treated differently from a real risotto made with rice. It is easier to cook because you do not need to keep stirring while adding the wine and stock, and there is no risk of overcooking. I often make double the quantity. When my granddaughter Ruby made it for a party with her friends at university she had one complaint, "There was not enough. Everyone wanted more."

You can make this in advance and heat it through before serving, but cook the asparagus at the last minute. The instructions on my package of barley say it takes 45 to 60 minutes, but it only takes about 30 minutes if the grain is soaked overnight. If you do soak it overnight, it will need less water – perhaps 1⅔ cups / 395ml.

Serves 4

1 cup / 180g pearl barley

2 tbsp olive oil

1 onion, chopped

2 cups / 480ml water, plus 7 tbsp / 100ml if needed

¾ cup / 175ml dry white wine

2 chicken or vegetable bouillon cubes

salt and black pepper

¾ cup / 200g frozen petite peas

4 to 5 tbsp / 60 to 75ml crème fraîche

grated zest of ½ lemon, plus 1 lemon, quartered

7 oz / 200g asparagus tips, trimmed and cut into pieces

grated Parmesan or Grana Padano for serving

Wash the barley in a bowl of cold water and rinse in a sieve under cold running water.

Warm the olive oil in a large pan over low heat and fry the onion, stirring often, for 5 to 8 minutes, until it is soft but not colored.

Pour in the 2 cups / 480ml water and the wine, add the bouillon cubes, and bring to a boil. Pour in the barley, cover, and simmer over low heat until the grain is tender, seasoning with salt and pepper midway during the cooking. It can take from 30 to 60 minutes, depending on the grain, if it was soaked overnight, and on how soft you like it. Add the 7 tbsp / 100ml water if it is dry. It should be very moist with a little liquid. (If you let it sit, the grain will absorb any remaining liquid and become softer.)

Cook the peas in boiling water for 5 minutes, then drain, keeping the cooking water. Using an immersion blender, blend the peas to a rough purée, adding about 5 tbsp / 75ml of the cooking water.

You can do all this in advance. Just before you are ready to serve, reheat the barley, adding a little water if needed. Reheat the pea purée and stir it into the barley with the crème fraîche and lemon zest.

While the barley is reheating, poach the asparagus pieces in salted water for 2 minutes, or until they are al dente, then drain. Serve the barley with the asparagus on top. Pass the lemon quarters and the grated cheese.

SPICED SAFFRON RICE

Since Roman times, Arabs were engaged as middlemen in the transport of spices and aromatics to Europe from the East. Each country on the route adopted favorites that have endured. You can serve this festive Arabian rice as a side with many dishes, and you must try the butternut squash or pumpkin variation below. It is the kind of dish I could imagine garnished with gold leaf in Renaissance Italy – something that is back in fashion today. Some basmati rice needs rinsing under cold water (check the package instructions).

Serves 6 to 8

3¾ cups / 890ml chicken or vegetable stock or water

½ tsp ground cardamom, or 12 cardamom pods, cracked

6 whole cloves

3 cinnamon sticks

½ tsp saffron threads, or 1 tsp ground turmeric

salt and black pepper

2½ cups / 500g basmati rice

5 tbsp / 75g butter, cut into pieces, or 3 tbsp sunflower oil

In a pan, bring the stock or water to a boil with the cardamom, cloves, and cinnamon sticks and simmer for 10 minutes.

Add the saffron or turmeric and a little salt and pepper to the pan and pour in the rice. Let come back to a boil, stir well, then turn the heat to low and cook, covered, for about 20 minutes, until little holes appear on the surface and the rice is tender. Stir in the butter or sunflower oil.

Serve the rice hot, in a mound.

Butternut squash or pumpkin pilaf

I buy butternut squash already peeled at the supermarket for this. Preheat the oven to 400°F. Cut 1 lb 10 oz / 750g butternut squash or pumpkin into ¾-inch cubes. Put in a baking dish, season with salt and black pepper, add 3 to 4 tbsp olive oil, and turn the pieces to coat all over, then bake for 40 to 45 minutes, turning them over once, until very tender and beginning to caramelize. Cover with foil if they are becoming too brown toward the end. Stir into the rice.

TURMERIC RICE WITH SPINACH AND YOGURT SAUCE

We thought our Aunt Regine was the most beautiful woman in Cairo. She loved beautiful things and delicate flavors. One of her recipes was a spinach and yogurt soup with rice and turmeric. I have turned it into a colorful and aromatic rice dish. Some basmati rice needs rinsing under cold water (check the package instructions).

Serves 6

4 cups / 950ml chicken or vegetable stock

1¼ tsp ground turmeric

salt

1½ cups / 300g long-grain or basmati rice

14 oz / 400g baby spinach, rinsed if necessary

7 tbsp / 100ml extra-virgin olive oil

juice of 1 lemon

black pepper

Yogurt sauce

2 cups / 500g plain yogurt

1 or 2 garlic cloves, crushed

grated zest of 1 lemon

Bring the stock to a boil in a pan over medium heat, stir in the turmeric, and season with salt. Pour in the rice, stir well, cover, and cook for 10 to 15 minutes (it varies depending on the type and quality of the rice, so check the package instructions), until it is only just tender. Don't let it get too soft. Add a little water if it becomes too dry before it is cooked, or drain if there is a lot of liquid left. Pour into a wide serving dish.

While the rice is cooking, put the spinach in a large pan. If you have rinsed them, they only need the water that clings to them. If they are dry, add 4 to 5 tbsp water. Put the lid on and cook over high heat for moments only, until the leaves crumple into a soft mass. Lift them out, leaving any liquid behind, and add them to the rice. Mix well and dress with a mixture of the extra-virgin olive oil and lemon juice and season with salt and pepper.

For the yogurt sauce, beat the yogurt with the garlic and lemon zest.

Serve the rice with the sauce on the side.

HERBED RICE WITH TOMATO "JAM"

Here, the rice is simply boiled, and just as it is about to be drained, a large amount of chopped fresh herbs are stirred in; they cling to the rice and stay very green and fresh. Choose two or more herbs, such as parsley, mint, chives, and dill.

This tomato sauce is inspired by a Moroccan relish, a confiture or "jam," so-called because it is thick and dense, sweet and aromatic with honey and rose water, with chile to mitigate the sweetness. I always make too much and keep any left over in the fridge to use with other dishes. Some basmati rice needs rinsing under cold water (check the package instructions).

Serves 4

Tomato "jam"

2 tbsp olive oil or sunflower oil

3 garlic cloves, crushed

two 14.5-oz / 411g cans diced tomatoes

2 tbsp honey

2 tbsp rose water (optional)

salt

Aleppo pepper, to taste

1¼ cups / 250g basmati or long-grain rice

1 large bunch herbs, leaves chopped

salt

3 tbsp extra-virgin olive oil

For the tomato "jam," in a wide sauté pan or skillet, warm the oil over low heat, add the garlic, and cook for a few seconds, stirring until the aroma rises and it just begins to color. Take the pan off the heat and pour in the tomatoes, then simmer, uncovered, over medium heat for about 25 minutes, until thick and jammy.

Stir in the honey and rose water (if using), season with salt and Aleppo pepper, and cook for 5 minutes over low heat. Pour into a bowl to pass around.

Cook the rice in plenty of boiling salted water for 10 to 15 minutes, stirring once, until tender (check the package instructions). Throw in the herbs, stir, and drain at once. Taste for salt and stir in the extra-virgin olive oil.

Serve the rice with the tomato "jam" alongside.

LENTILS AND RICE WITH DATES AND CARAMELIZED ONIONS

When my parents settled in London, my mother, missing her family, her friends, and her old life, threw herself into cooking. In Egypt she had left it to the cook; in London it was a passion. To please my father, she cooked the remembered dishes of his childhood. This is the Egyptian megadarra he loved – with added dates.

The lentils you get in supermarkets do not need soaking and take no more than 20 minutes to cook, so you can cook them together with the rice, but check the package instructions, especially for the rice, as cooking times can vary. This is traditionally a first course to be eaten at room temperature; but with the optional accompaniments, it is the star of a vegetarian Middle Eastern meal.

Serves 4 to 6

6 tbsp / 90ml olive oil

2 large onions, halved and thickly sliced

scant 1 cup / 180g brown or green lentils, rinsed

salt

1 cup / 200g basmati rice, rinsed

1 tsp ground cinnamon

¼ tsp ground allspice

black pepper

12 pitted soft dried dates, such as Medjool, coarsely chopped

Accompaniments (optional)

9 oz / 260g halloumi cheese, cut into 8 slices

1 lemon, cut into wedges

labneh (see page 45), or 2 cups / 480g Greek yogurt mixed with salt and 1 crushed garlic clove

Tomato "jam" (see page 155)

Cucumber and tomato salad (page 84)

In a wide skillet over low heat, warm 2 tbsp of the olive oil and fry the onions, stirring often. Start with the lid on, and when the onions are very soft continue over medium heat until they are really dark brown – not black or burned – about 25 minutes. Set aside.

Bring 7⅔ cups / 1.8L water to a boil and throw in the lentils. Simmer for 10 minutes, season with salt, then throw in the rice, add the cinnamon and allspice, and cook for 10 to 15 minutes, until the rice and lentils are tender.

Drain and pour the rice and lentils into a wide serving dish. Season with salt (it needs a lot) and pepper, then stir in the dates and remaining 4 tbsp / 60ml olive oil. Mix very gently, turning over with a spatula, so as not to break the grains of rice.

If you like, cook the halloumi slices on an oiled grill pan or nonstick skillet over medium-high heat until browned on both sides. Do this just before serving so that the cheese is still very hot and soft, as it becomes rubbery when it cools.

Serve the lentils and rice warm or at room temperature, sprinkled with the caramelized onions, along with any or all of the optional accompaniments.

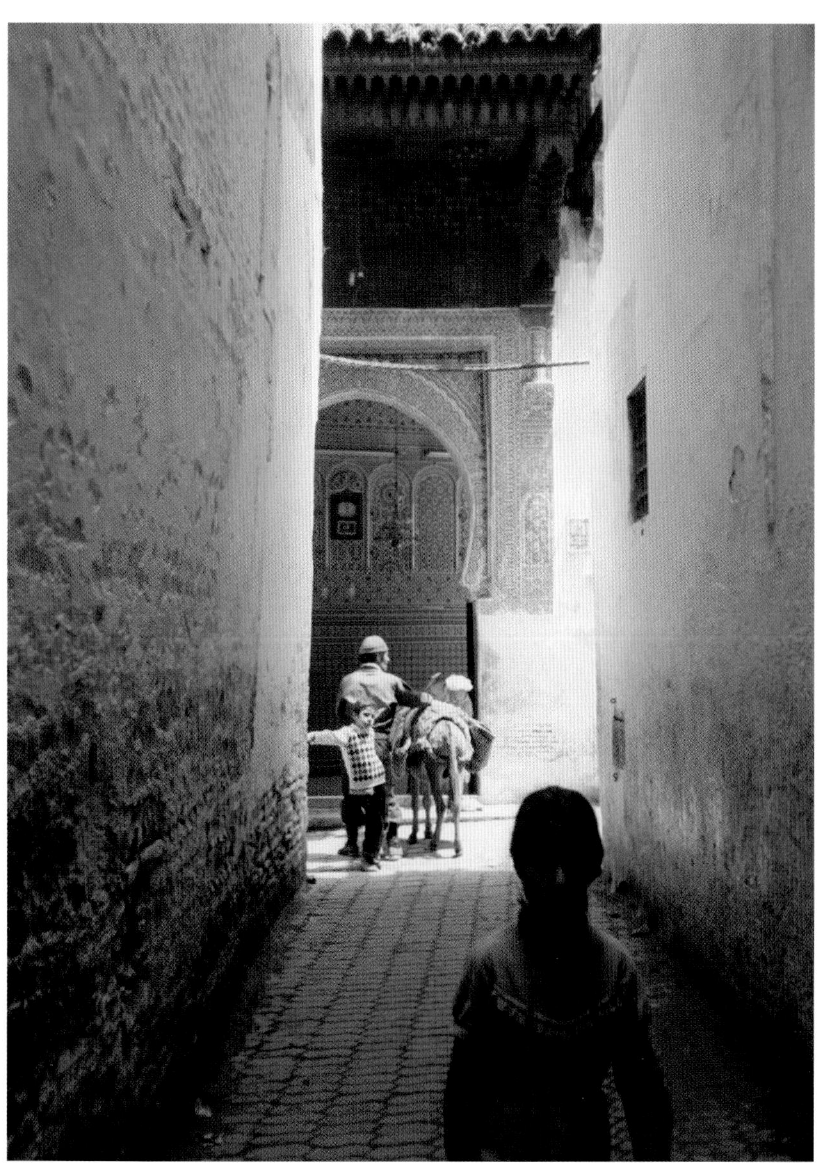

BULGUR PILAF WITH CHICKPEAS, EGGPLANTS, AND TOMATOES

This rich Levantine combination is immensely satisfying, with layers of flavor and aroma. The optional halloumi cheese makes it a meal in itself. Accompany if you like with Greek yogurt and cucumber and tomato salad (page 84). As with anything cooked with oil, leftovers can be eaten cold – but you'll want to reheat if there is halloumi, as the cheese becomes rubbery when cold.

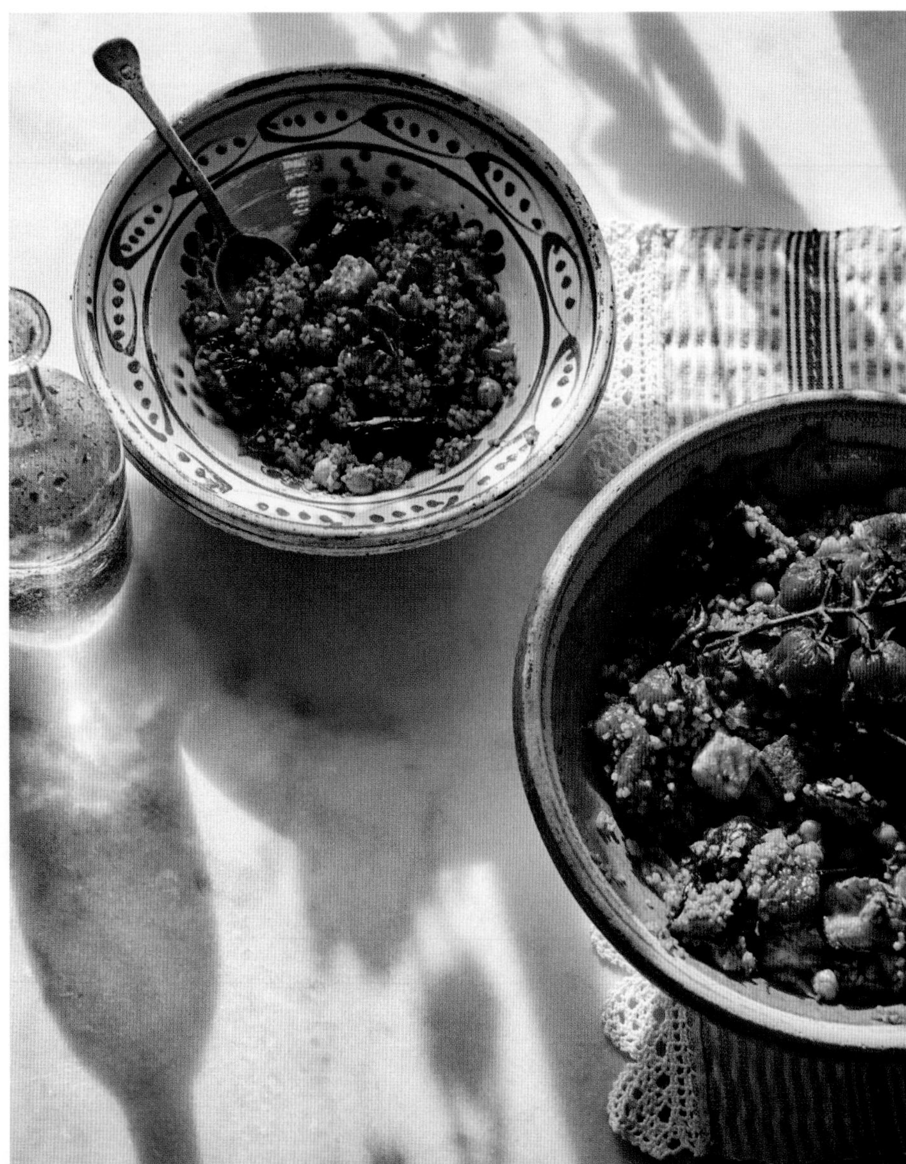

Serves 6 to 8

6 tbsp / 90ml olive oil

2 eggplants, trimmed and cut into 1¼-inch cubes

salt and black pepper

10 oz / 285g cherry or Santini tomatoes

2 onions, chopped

3 garlic cloves, chopped

2¼ cups / 360g bulgur

one 14-oz / 397g can chickpeas, drained and rinsed

1½ to 2 tbsp tomato paste

1 tsp ground cinnamon

½ tsp ground allspice

1 tsp ground cumin

1 good pinch Aleppo pepper

2 cups / 480ml boiling water

two 8.8-oz / 250g packages halloumi cheese (optional)

3 tbsp extra-virgin olive oil

Warm 3 tbsp of the olive oil in a sauté pan with a tight-fitting lid over medium heat. Add the eggplants and cook, turning the cubes over with a spatula so that all have a few minutes to get browned, season with salt and pepper, and put the lid back on so that they steam in their own juice for about 15 minutes. Add the cherry tomatoes, turn them over with the eggplant, then continue to cook, covered, for about 8 minutes, until soft and beginning to release some juice.

In a large pan over medium heat, warm 2 tbsp olive oil and fry the onions for 8 minutes, stirring often, until soft and beginning to color. Add the garlic and cook, stirring, for 2 minutes, until the aroma rises and it begins to color. Take off the heat and stir in the bulgur and chickpeas.

Put the tomato paste into a liquid measuring cup and add the cinnamon, allspice, cumin, Aleppo pepper, and some salt. Pour in the boiling water and stir vigorously, then pour into the pan with the bulgur and mix well. Bring to a boil, cover, and cook over low heat for 15 minutes. Taste for salt, you will probably need more.

If adding the halloumi, cut the cheese into 1¼-inch cubes and cook quickly with the remaining 1 tbsp olive oil in a nonstick skillet over medium-high heat, turning the pieces to brown them all over. Mix into the bulgur.

Turn the bulgur into a large baking dish and mix in the eggplant and tomatoes. Serve with the extra-virgin olive oil drizzled over.

TAGLIOLINI WITH LEMON

Many Italian dishes have a squeeze of lemon or a hint of its zest, but in these incredibly delicious Sicilian tagliolini al limone, lemon is the star. Everybody loves this. Serve as a first course.

Serves 2 to 4

7 oz / 200g tagliolini
grated zest and juice of 1 lemon
6 tbsp / 90ml heavy cream
salt
black pepper
grated Parmesan or Grana Padano for serving

Cook the tagliolini in boiling salted water according to the package instructions.

In a serving bowl, mix the lemon zest and juice with the cream and season with salt.

When the pasta is cooked al dente, drain and mix with the lemon sauce. Let everyone help themselves to sprinkle with pepper and cheese.

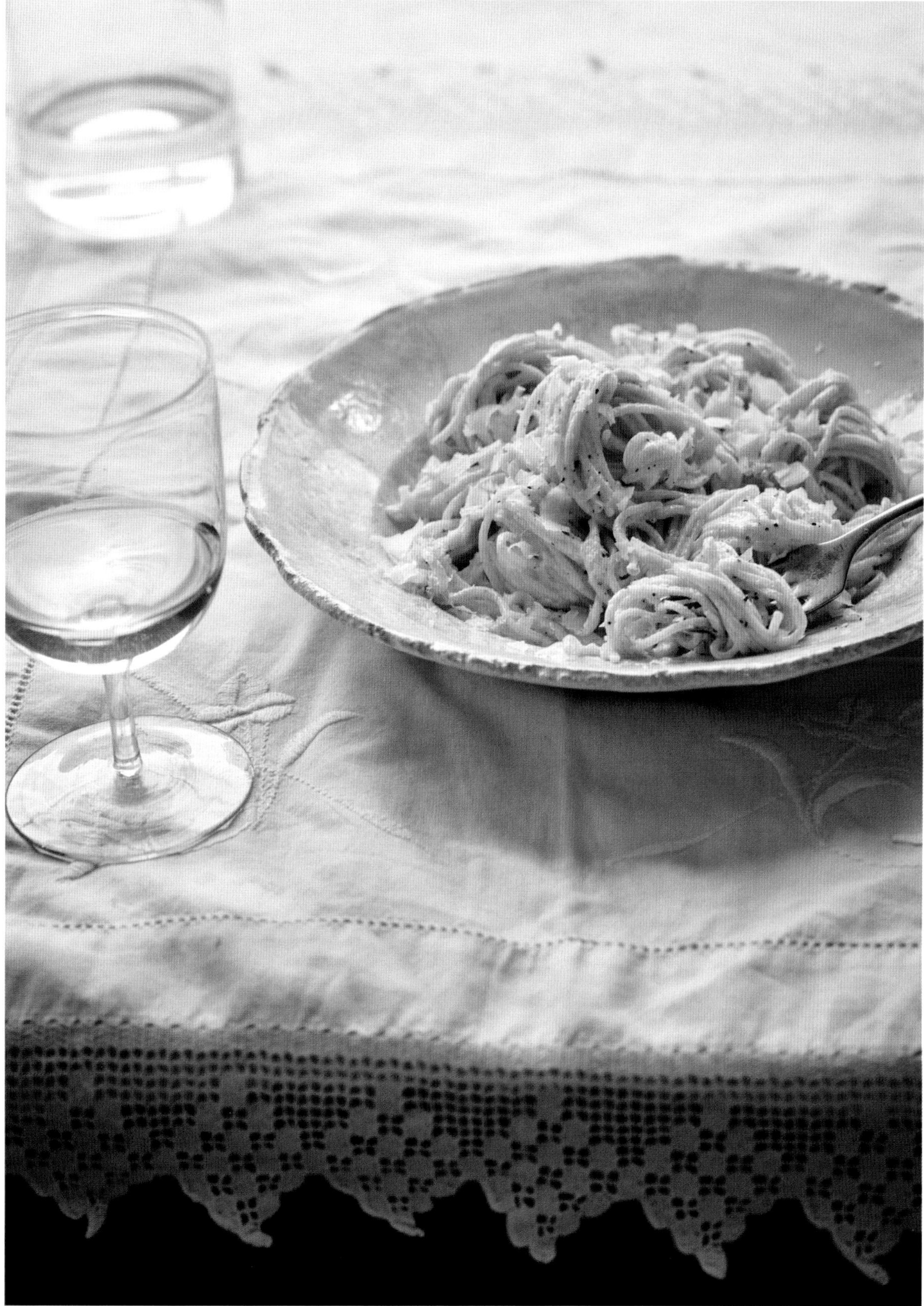

MALLOREDDUS AL CAPRINO FRESCO

At a hunting lodge in Sardinia, I was the only other person in the dining room when a large group of hunters – all men who were singing loudly – invited me to join them at their table. The hostess promptly told me to go back to my own table and to leave the next day. She had already chased me out of the kitchen that morning, even though I showed her a letter from a newspaper saying I was writing a piece for them. The cooks were making malloreddus, the conch-shaped ridged Sardinian pasta, with caprino cheese for their own meal. It is delicious but very rich; I serve a small amount for a first course. You can use ridged penne instead, because they, too, will hold the creamy sauce well. Saffron, another product of Sardinia, is optional.

Serves 4

7 oz / 200g malloreddus or ridged penne
9 oz / 255g fresh soft goat cheese
grated zest of ½ lemon
grated zest of ½ orange
salt and black pepper
1 pinch saffron threads (optional)

Cook the pasta in boiling salted water according to the package instructions.

Mash the cheese with a fork in a wide pan. Add the grated citrus zests, season with salt and pepper, and stir in 1 to 2 tbsp of the boiling pasta water. If using the saffron, put it in a small bowl or cup and add 2 tbsp of the boiling pasta water; let infuse for 2 to 3 minutes, then add to the cheese. Stir vigorously to make a creamy sauce. Heat gently when the pasta is ready.

When the pasta is cooked al dente, drain, reserving 1 to 2 tbsp of the cooking water. Transfer to the pan with the cheese and mix well, adding the reserved cooking water so that the sauce is creamy. Serve hot.

SPAGHETTI WITH GARLIC, OIL, AND CHILE

I have a special fondness for this simple dish because I first tasted it when I was a student at Saint Martin's School of Art in London, and sculptor Eduardo Paolozzi invited a few of us to eat it at his studio. We were enthralled. Many years later, when I spent time in the kitchen of a hotel in Sicily that specialized in wedding parties, the tired chefs – at the end of their day preparing extraordinarily rich banquets – sat together and ate pasta aglio and olio e peperoncino.

Serves 4 to 6

14 oz / 400g spaghetti

7 tbsp / 100ml extra-virgin olive oil

5 garlic cloves, finely chopped

2 fresh red chiles, seeded and finely chopped

salt

1 bunch flat-leaf parsley, leaves chopped

Cook the pasta in plenty of boiling salted water. Warm 3 tbsp of the olive oil in a saucepan over medium heat. Add the garlic and chiles and cook, stirring until the aroma rises and the garlic only just begins to color. Remove from the heat and stir in the remaining 4 tbsp / 60ml oil.

When the pasta is cooked al dente, drain and transfer to the pan with the sauce. Toss thoroughly, seasoning with salt and sprinkling with the parsley. Serve hot.

Variation

Other herbs, such as basil and mint, are sometimes added with the parsley. A chef in Trapani, Sicily, said he used thirteen, including marjoram, oregano, thyme, sage, and rosemary, and called it spaghetti alle erbe. I didn't believe him. However, you might like to add a few.

SPAGHETTI WITH ANCHOVIES AND OLIVES

In Naples and Sicily, they have an aristocratic cucina nobile, but it is their cucina povera (*povera* means "poor") that has the richest flavors. These spaghetti poveri are for anchovy lovers, like me. I often make it for myself and have all the ingredients on hand in the pantry. Use good-tasting olives, such as Italian Taggiasche or Greek Kalamata.

Serves 3

9 oz / 255g spaghetti

6 tbsp / 90ml extra-virgin olive oil

4 to 5 garlic cloves, chopped

½ to 1 fresh hot red chile, seeded and finely chopped, or 1 good pinch Aleppo pepper

2¼ oz / 60g anchovy fillets, drained and chopped

3½ oz / 100g pitted black olives, cut into pieces

1 bunch flat-leaf parsley, leaves chopped

Cook the pasta in plenty of boiling salted water. In a wide skillet over low heat, warm 2 tbsp of the olive oil. Add the garlic and cook for a few seconds, until the aroma rises. Add the chile or Aleppo pepper and anchovies and cook, stirring until the anchovies melt into the oil. Take off the heat and stir in the olives and parsley.

When the pasta is cooked al dente, drain and transfer to the pan with the sauce. Add the remaining 4 tbsp / 60ml olive oil and mix very well. Serve hot.

PASTA WITH FRESH TOMATOES, GARLIC, AND BASIL

A British magazine had arranged for me to telephone Italian celebrities and ask them for their favorite pasta recipe. Luciano Pavarotti was in a hotel in New York when I rang him. It was electrifying to hear him describe this dish that he cooked for himself. For a long time, whenever I cooked an Italian dish, I played his "O sole mio" and other Neapolitan songs.

Serves 2

2 tbsp extra-virgin olive oil

2 to 4 garlic cloves, finely chopped

1 lb / 450g ripe plum tomatoes, peeled and chopped

½ tsp sugar, or to taste

salt and black pepper

2 tbsp torn fresh basil leaves

7 oz / 200g spaghetti

grated Parmesan, Pecorino sardo, or Grana Padano for serving

Warm the olive oil in a skillet over medium heat. Add the garlic and fry, until it just begins to color. Stir in the tomatoes and sugar, season with salt and pepper, then simmer for 8 minutes. Take off the heat and stir in the basil.

Cook the pasta in boiling salted water according to the package instructions until al dente, then drain and toss with the sauce.

Serve the pasta with grated cheese.

SEAFOOD AND SHELLFISH

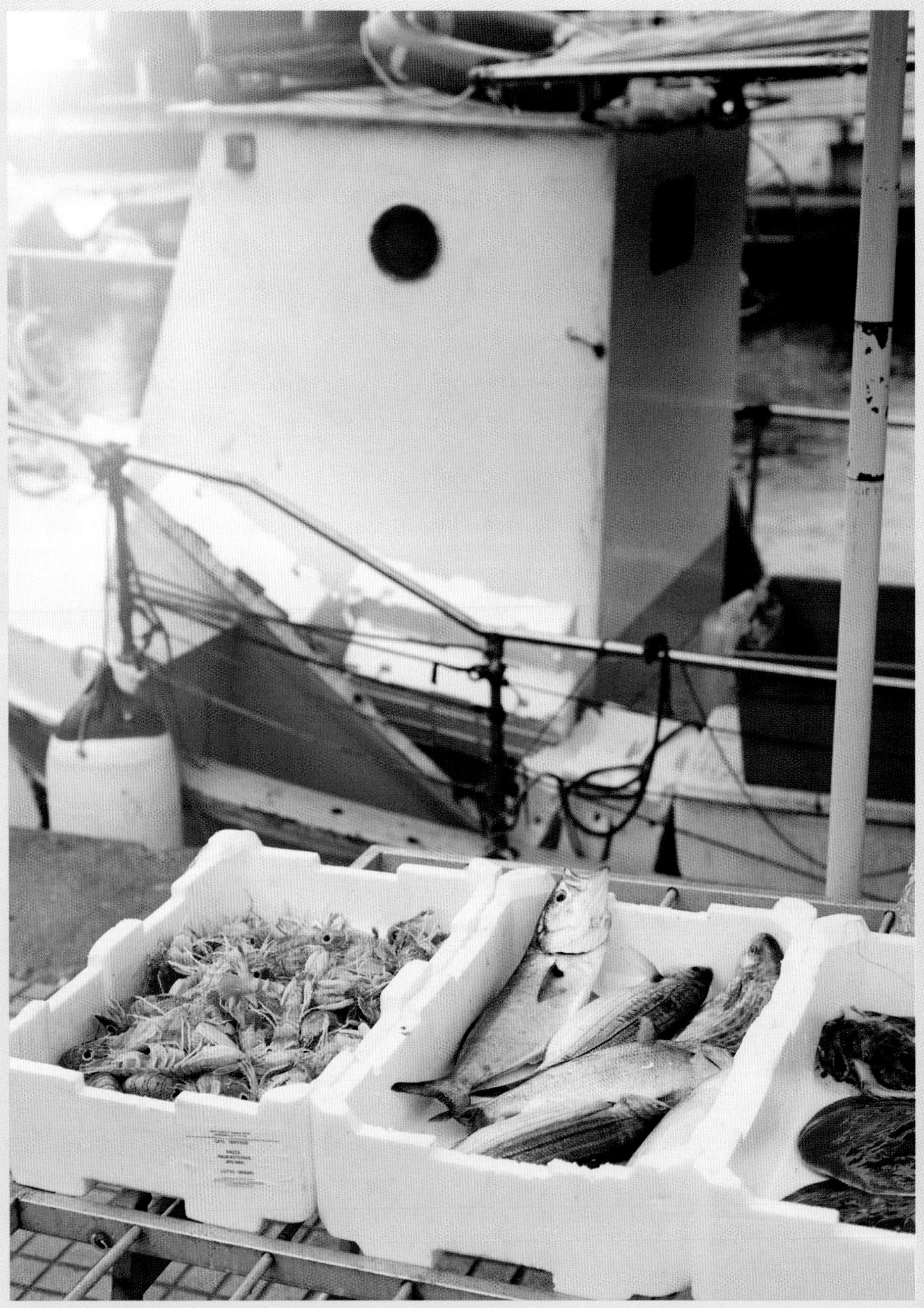

Until the early twentieth century, fish was considered food for the poor in Mediterranean countries. The wealthy and aristocratic were only interested in meat. Because of the high mountains and lack of transport in the hinterland, before roads were built and before refrigeration, the only fish available in the interior was from rivers – trout, salmon, and eels – or salted cod. Fishermen could barely sell their fish; they fished for their own consumption. Many of the glorious seafood dishes that developed with tourism are said to be inspired by what they cooked for themselves on boats or brought home for their wives to prepare. Fish soups especially, born from the leftovers of their catch, are seen as having gone from "poor" to "posh." You only have to see the eager faces of people queuing at fish stalls in markets, who watch the fishmonger clean, fillet, and prepare their wares with art and tenderness, to understand just how important and appreciated fish and shellfish have become.

Mediterranean fishermen are often of mixed ethnic ancestry – Genoese, Neapolitan, Sicilian, Spanish, Greek, Tunisian – because they moved around. In Sicily, Arabic words have been used in tuna fishing since early medieval times, and the port city of Trapani, famous for its fish couscous, has a Tunisian quarter, while a neighboring fishing village has one called la casbah, which is home to a Tunisian community. In Sardinia, fishermen still speak thirteenth-century Catalan. In Gibraltar, many people have Genoese names because of the Genoese fishermen who settled there. I once planned a menu for the Gibraltar Literary Festival around the influences on Gibraltarian gastronomy. We had a dinner in advance in London to try the dishes and I spoke a few words about the origin of each dish. When I explained the Genoese legacy, the Gibraltarian High Commissioner, who was there, told us that his grandfather had been a fisherman from Genoa. This is also the reason why you can find similar fish dishes with similar-sounding names throughout the region.

The cities dotted all along the Mediterranean coastline like a necklace – the bustling seaports and fishing villages with their marinas and fish auctions, squares, markets, and cafés; the mixtures of people and cultures – are vibrant living proof of the unity and diversity of the Mediterranean universe that is so attractive to me. The dishes in this chapter are those that stayed with me, that I want to keep making for my friends and family.

EASY AÏOLI

The aïoli of Provence and its variations are served with many fish and shellfish dishes. I once made this garlicky mayonnaise with a mortar and pestle – it was laborious, but satisfying – and for years I made it with a simple whisk, not always successfully. When I saw someone make it with an immersion blender in a tall thin beaker, I couldn't believe it. This extremely easy way of making mayonnaise in a few minutes works perfectly. Hurray!

Makes 1¼ cups / 300ml

1 egg
1 tbsp lemon juice
2 to 4 garlic cloves, to taste, crushed
1 pinch salt
¾ cup plus 2 tbsp / 200ml sunflower oil
3 tbsp extra-virgin olive oil

Make sure everything is at room temperature – this is important. Remove the egg from the fridge 1 hour before you start.

Put the egg, lemon juice, garlic, and salt in a large liquid measuring cup and pour in both oils. They will remain on top.

Put the immersion blender right down to the bottom of the measuring cup and turn it on. Keep it down until the mixture becomes a pale thick cream that rises in the oil. Gently move the blender, still running, up and down until all the oil has been incorporated into a thick aïoli.

Transfer the aïoli to a bowl and keep, covered, in the fridge for up to 2 weeks.

Variations

~ For rouille, add 1 to 2 tsp paprika or sweet pimentón and a good pinch of cayenne, or 1 tbsp harissa.

~ For saffron aïoli, heat a good pinch of saffron threads in 1 tbsp water and stir into the aïoli.

~ For green aïoli, add chopped herbs such as dill, chives, basil, mint, and parsley.

~ For tomato aïoli, beat in 2 tbsp tomato paste.

Making aïoli with good-quality mayonnaise

If you do not want to use raw egg, substitute 1¼ cups / 300ml good-quality "real" mayonnaise and beat in 3 tbsp extra-virgin olive oil, the juice of ½ lemon, and two to four crushed garlic cloves. You can also make the variations in the same way.

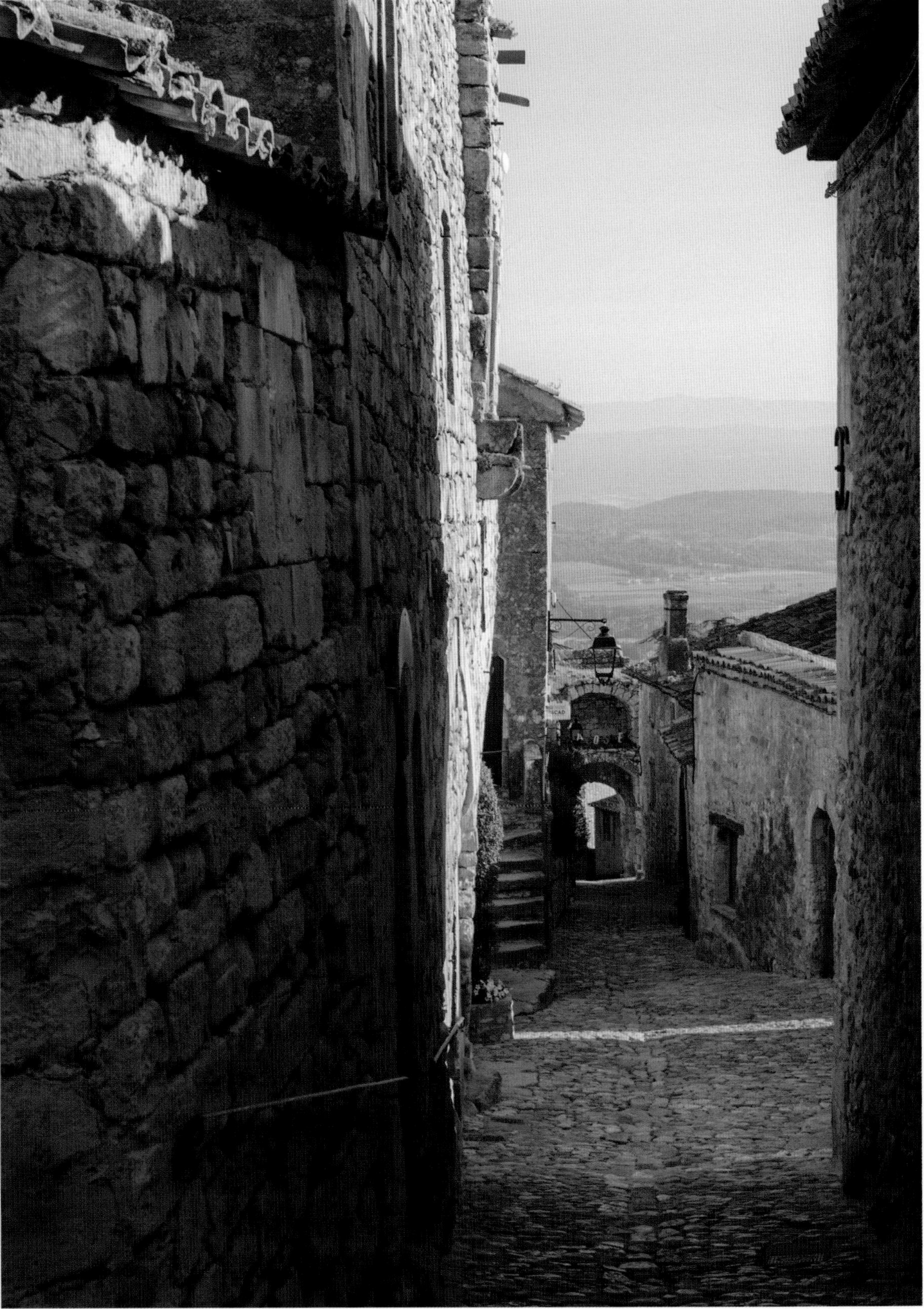

LE GRAND AÏOLI

The French flag bunting around the square, the band playing bal-musette tango and polka, the long trestle table covered with paper, everyone helping themselves to salt cod, boiled vegetables, hard-boiled eggs, and masses of shining aïoli. Can my aïoli dinner ever taste as good as the one that day at the fête du village in Lacoste in the Vaucluse? It does bring joy. The aïoli is the star. The usual vegetables are potatoes, carrots, and green beans, but you can add others such as cauliflower, fennel, artichoke hearts, broccoli, and zucchini. And fresh cod will do instead of salt cod.

Serves 6

6 waxy potatoes, scrubbed

6 carrots, peeled

salt

1 lb 5 oz / 595g green beans, trimmed

1 cauliflower, trimmed and cut into 6 pieces

6 hard-boiled eggs, cut in half lengthwise

6 skinless cod loin fillets (about 1 lb 10 oz / 740g total weight)

2½ cups / 600ml aïoli (see page 174)

extra-virgin olive oil for serving

flaky sea salt and black pepper

If you have a large enough pan, you can cook all the vegetables together. Add the potatoes and carrots, cover with plenty of water, season with salt, and bring to a boil. Simmer for 15 minutes, then add the green beans and cauliflower and simmer for 6 to 8 minutes, until all the vegetables are tender. Drain and divide among two large platters, then top with the eggs.

Bring another pan of salted water to a gentle simmer and poach the fish for 2 to 5 minutes, until the flesh begins to flake. Drain and divide among the platters with the vegetables.

Serve hot or warm. Pass around the aïoli and olive oil for people to help themselves. Have tiny bowls of flaky sea salt and a pepper mill on the table.

SEAFOOD GELATIN

I was judging the best restaurant in Australia and worrying about the impossibility of deciding. Then, I had a dish called "Rockpool" at Stephanie Alexander's in Melbourne. What you do with the memory of a dish often turns out to be entirely different from the one that inspired you. The flavors of my seafood gelatin are those of Marseille and bouillabaisse. It is different every time I make it. Use seafood that you like, and can afford. It is not a firm jellied terrine that you unmold – it is soft. Make it in a wide serving dish and let it set in the fridge for at least 4 hours, or overnight. It is one of my grand, very beautiful dishes.

Serve it with a homemade saffron aïoli or rouille (see pages 174 to 175), or with a good-quality mayonnaise. If you can't buy good fresh fish stock, use a fish or seafood bouillon base.

Serves 6 to 8

4 cups / 950ml fish stock

½ cup / 120ml dry white wine

9 oz / 255g skinless white fish fillets, such as cod or monkfish

9 oz / 255g raw peeled tiger prawns

7 oz / 200g small wild Atlantic scallops

3 thyme sprigs, leaves only

2 bay leaves

1 tsp fennel seeds

strips of peel from ½ orange

1 pinch saffron threads or good-quality saffron powder

1 tbsp lemon juice

1 tsp sugar

3 tbsp anise-flavored spirit such as pastis, arak, raki, or ouzo (optional)

2¼ tsp unflavored gelatin

5 tbsp / 75ml cold water

1 bunch flat-leaf parsley, leaves chopped

1 small bunch dill, chopped

In a large pan, bring the fish stock and white wine to a gentle simmer. Very briefly poach the seafood, one type at a time, until barely cooked – the fish until it just begins to flake when you cut into it, the prawns until they turn pink, the scallops for seconds only (they are best when they are slightly underdone). Lift them out with a slotted spoon and set them aside.

Add the thyme, bay leaves, fennel seeds, orange peel, saffron, lemon juice, sugar, and anise-flavored spirit (if using) to the fish stock. Cover and simmer over low heat for 15 to 20 minutes, tasting to check the seasoning. Strain the liquid through a fine-mesh sieve into a large measuring cup; it should come up to about 3½ cups / 830ml. If not, add a little water and check the seasoning again. Return to the pan and heat through, then turn off the heat and let it cool for 10 minutes.

In a bowl, sprinkle the gelatin over the cold water and set aside for 5 minutes – it will swell slightly and become soft. Add the softened gelatin to the hot fish stock and stir vigorously until it has dissolved.

Rinse a wide serving dish or bowl with water and pour in the stock. Add the seafood, parsley, and dill and mix gently. Let cool, then cover and leave in the fridge for at least 4 hours, or overnight, until set.

Serve chilled or at room temperature.

FISH TARTARE WITH TOMATO VINAIGRETTE

Raw salmon dressed with a Catalan vinagreta de tomàquet and accompanied by a little bowl of mayonnaise (see below) is heaven. In Arab culinary lore, I have often encountered dishes "you make when you love somebody." This is one such dish for me.

You must use ultrafresh fish – not from a supermarket. I get my salmon from my local Japanese mini market, where they sell it sliced for sashimi or will slice it for you. Buy the fish on the day you want to serve it and keep it covered in the fridge until you are ready to serve.

Serves 4

¼ cup / 60ml mild fruity extra-virgin olive oil

grated zest of 1 lemon, plus juice of ½ lemon

½ tsp honey

salt and black pepper

1 large beefsteak tomato

10 oz / 285g very fresh raw salmon, sliced for sashimi

2 handfuls baby salad greens

2 tbsp snipped fresh chives

2 tbsp chopped fresh dill

Put the olive oil in a bowl; add the lemon zest, lemon juice, and honey; season with salt and pepper; and beat well with a fork. Cut the tomato in half crosswise and grate through the large holes of a box grater into the bowl, pressing hard and leaving the skin behind. Stir with the fork to mix the tomato with the dressing.

Arrange the salmon slices on individual plates with some salad greens on the side. Pour on the dressing and sprinkle with the chives and dill before serving.

Lemon and chili garlic mayonnaise

Beat 7 tbsp / 100ml good-quality mayonnaise with 1 tbsp lemon juice, a crushed garlic clove, and a pinch of Aleppo pepper or cayenne pepper. Alternatively, use 7 tbsp / 100ml homemade aïoli (see page 174).

CRAB SALAD

My mother's cool and glamorous cousin Edith, who lived in the Swiss Cottage area of London, asked, "Do you want a crab?" I had gone to see her for family recipes, but crab was not one of them. She took me to the fishmonger, where she bought a large live crab. I have eaten and cooked many crabs since – crabcakes, gratins, salads – but it's the simplicity of Edith's crab salad that is so appealing.

You can buy jumbo lump crabmeat in supermarkets; it is expensive but worth it. It has such a delicate flavor that you need a mild extra-virgin olive oil.

Serves 2

2¾ oz / 80g jumbo lump crabmeat
1 handful arugula leaves
1 tomato, finely diced
1 green onion (white part), sliced
½ to 1 tbsp lemon juice
2 tbsp mild extra-virgin olive oil
salt and black pepper
1 tbsp chopped flat-leaf parsley

Divide the crabmeat among two plates and arrange the arugula, diced tomato, and green onion around it.

Whisk together the lemon juice and olive oil, season with salt and pepper, and dress the salad.

Serve the salad sprinkled with the parsley.

HARICOT BEANS WITH CLAMS

One night on the seafront in Barcelona, I was looking for a restaurant that served zarzuela. I had eaten the extraordinary seafood stew many years before and it had left such an impression that I was desperately keen to have it again. My friend Pepa Aymami, who lives in Barcelona, only wanted clams. My zarzuela was disappointing but Pepa's clams were delicious.

The Spanish alubias con almejas is my favorite clam recipe. Use good-quality white haricot beans from a can. The wine gives them a delicate flavor and the clams add the taste of the sea.

Serves 2

1 lb 8 oz / 680g clams

3 tbsp olive oil

1 large onion, chopped

½ small fresh red chile, chopped (optional)

3 to 4 garlic cloves, finely chopped

one 15-oz / 425g can small white haricot beans or Great Northern beans, drained and rinsed

1 cup / 120ml fruity white wine or cava

salt

2 tbsp chopped flat-leaf parsley

Throw away any clams that are broken and any open ones that do not close when you tap them on the sink or dip them in ice-cold water. Scrub them with a brush if they are dirty, then leave in fresh cold water for 20 minutes – they will push out any sand that remains inside. Lift them out and rinse them in cold water.

Warm the olive oil in a wide Dutch oven or pan with a tight-fitting lid over low heat. Add the onion and the chile (if using) and stir until very soft and beginning to color. Add the garlic and stir for a minute or so.

Add the beans, wine or cava, and a little salt to the pan; mix gently; and cook for 2 to 3 minutes. Put the clams on top, put the lid on, and cook over medium-high heat for 2 to 3 minutes, until the clams open. Throw away any that do not open. Serve sprinkled with the parsley.

OCTOPUS IN RED WINE AND POTATO SALAD

It was late summer on the Greek island of Skopelos. Men were bashing octopus on rocks to tenderize them and then hanging them up on lines. As I was walking past a family eating on their terrace, they invited me in to share their octopus salad and a bottle of wine. It was heaven. In my version, cooked in red wine, the octopus acquires a delicate flavor and rich color.

Octopuses are usually sold cleaned and often frozen (freezing tenderizes them). A 2¼-lb / 1kg octopus might look huge when you buy it, but it will shrink enormously when you cook it. Thaw it completely before cooking – you can let it sit overnight in the fridge.

Serves 6

1 octopus (about 2¼ lb / 1kg), thawed if frozen

1¼ cups / 300ml red wine

2 tbsp wine vinegar

2 tsp sugar

salt and black pepper

1 lb / 450g waxy new potatoes

6 tbsp / 90ml extra-virgin olive oil

2 tbsp lemon juice

1 good pinch Aleppo pepper (optional)

1 tbsp chopped flat-leaf parsley

Wash the octopus under cold running water inside and out. Cut away the head and cut out the central beak, if it has not already been removed, and throw them away. Half-fill a very large pan with water and bring to a boil. Throw in the octopus and blanch for 3 minutes, until it firms and the tentacles curl up gracefully, then drain.

Put the octopus back in the empty pan and add the wine, vinegar, and sugar and season with salt and pepper. Add just enough water to cover and simmer gently for 45 to 60 minutes, until the top of a tentacle feels very tender when you pierce it with a knife. Let cool in the cooking broth, then drain. Lift it out of the pan and cut the tentacles into 1¼-inch pieces, leaving the thin ends longer.

While the octopus is cooking, peel the potatoes and cook them in boiling salted water until tender. Drain and cut them into slices about ½ inch thick.

Beat the olive oil with the lemon juice and Aleppo pepper (if using). Season with salt and black pepper. Dress the potatoes and the octopus pieces separately, using half of the mixture for each. Mix them together and serve at room temperature, sprinkled with the parsley.

CREAMED SALT COD, POTATOES, AND GARLIC

Even when they lived by the sea, many people I spoke to said their favorite fish was salt cod – *brandade* in France, *baccalà* in Italy, and *bacalao* in Spain and Portugal.

Cod is not a fish of Mediterranean waters and you may wonder why a dried fish is so popular in coastal areas. Since the tenth century, fishermen have been going out to the North Atlantic to get cod. They fillet it on their boats, stack the fillets between layers of salt to extract the moisture, and dry them. The Christian countries became dedicated to the strong, distinctive taste when the fish was used as a replacement for meat during Lent and other fasting days, at a time when fresh fish was unobtainable in the interior due to lack of transport and refrigeration. The old traditional penitential dishes are now much-loved delicacies.

You can find salt cod in Italian stores and in some supermarkets. It needs to be soaked in cold water for around 24 hours before you can use it.

My very favorite salt cod dish is brandade. I used to buy it from the market in the Rue de Seine in Paris and eat it, still hot, sitting on a bench in a little garden where people went to scatter bread for birds.

Serve as an appetizer spread on small pieces of thin toast brushed with extra-virgin olive oil, or as a first course accompanied by a green salad.

Serves 6

10 oz / 285g salt cod

2 large baking potatoes, peeled and quartered

½ cup / 120ml heavy cream or whole milk, warmed

½ cup / 120ml extra-virgin olive oil

1 to 3 garlic cloves, to taste

black pepper

salt

juice of ½ lemon (optional)

2 to 3 tbsp snipped fresh chives (optional)

Soak the salt cod in plenty of cold water for 24 hours, changing the water at least four times. Drain before using.

Boil the potatoes in salted water until soft, then drain.

Place the drained salt cod in a pan of cold water and bring to a simmer, then remove the pan from the heat and let it stand for 15 minutes. Drain, then carefully remove any skin and bones (there are usually quite a few) and flake into small pieces with your fingers.

Put the fish in a food processor and blend to a paste. Then pour in the cream or milk and olive oil, a little at a time, alternating them, and pulse to a creamy paste.

Add the garlic to the cod and season with pepper, then add the boiled potatoes and blend to a purée that retains a little texture. If you have oversoaked the fish and desalted it too much, you may need to add a little salt. You may also like to add a little lemon juice.

If serving cold, spoon into a bowl and sprinkle with the chives (if using). If you want to serve it hot, preheat the oven to 350°F. Spoon the mixture into a baking dish and bake for 10 minutes.

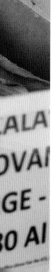

BABY SQUID IN THEIR INK WITH VERMICELLI AND AÏOLI

I discovered short, thin pasta cooked with seafood in a paella pan on the Valencian coast of Spain, where my friend Alicia Ríos had a house overlooking the sea. My favorite version is the mesmerizing chipirones en su tinta con fideus – short, thin pasta in a shiny black sauce with tiny squid and a fantastic taste of the sea. It is easy to make. I use dried vermicelli nests, but you can also use short, thin wheat noodles.

Many fishmongers and some supermarkets sell frozen packs of baby squid not more than 3 inches long, cleaned and packed with the tentacles inside the bodies. Some also sell sachets of concentrated cuttlefish or squid ink.

Serves 4

One 1¾-lb / 800g package frozen prepared baby squid, thawed

4 tbsp / 60ml olive oil

1 large onion, chopped

2 garlic cloves, crushed

1 very large or 2 medium tomatoes, peeled and chopped

⅔ cup / 160ml dry white wine

scant 2 cups / 450ml fish stock

½ tsp sugar

salt and black pepper

2 to 3 sachets squid ink

7 oz / 200g dried vermicelli nests or short fine wheat noodles

2 tbsp chopped flat-leaf parsley (optional)

aïoli (see page 174) for serving

Drain the thawed squid, take the tentacles out of the bodies, and slice the bodies into rings about ⅜ inch wide.

In a large pan over low heat, warm 2 tbsp of the olive oil. Fry the onion, covered with a lid but stirring often, for 10 to 15 minutes, until soft and golden. Add the garlic and cook, stirring, until the aroma rises and it just begins to color. Add the tomato and cook for 5 to 8 minutes, stirring often, then add the wine, fish stock, sugar, and some salt (taking into consideration the saltiness of the fish stock) and pepper. Simmer over low heat for 10 minutes, then add the squid ink (3 sachets will make the sauce blacker).

In a large skillet over medium heat, warm the remaining 2 tbsp olive oil and fry the squid rings and tentacles for about 10 minutes, stirring and turning the pieces over.

Crush the vermicelli into small pieces and throw them into the ink sauce. Cook for 3 to 6 minutes, with the lid on, stirring often, until done. Add the squid rings and tentacles, scatter with the parsley, if using, and serve hot, with aïoli.

SPAGHETTI WITH PRAWNS PROVENÇAL

There are many versions of pasta with seafood around the Mediterranean sea. When, for an assignment, I asked Italian celebrities what their favorite pasta dish was, most said "ai frutti di mare" and that it was their own recipe. I tried the recipes and loved them all. But for *my* favorite, I cook the pasta a Catalan way in boiling fish stock (it adds a surprise layer of flavor) and serve with a sauce from the Côte d'Azur. My grandson Cesar, a pasta man, adds a lot of chile heat. I sometimes add other seafood, such as squid or shellfish.

Serves 4

1 lb / 450g ripe tomatoes
1 onion, chopped
2 tbsp olive oil
3 garlic cloves, chopped
¾ cup / 175ml dry white wine
3 thyme sprigs, leaves only
1 to 2 tsp sugar
1 good pinch Aleppo pepper
salt
1 lb / 450g raw peeled tiger prawns
2 fish stock cubes
14 oz / 400g spaghetti
2 tbsp extra-virgin olive oil
3 tbsp chopped flat-leaf parsley

Quarter the tomatoes and remove the little white hard bits at the stem end. Blend them to a creamy consistency in a food processor.

In a wide pan over low heat, fry the onion in the olive oil, stirring often, until it is very soft. Add the garlic, and when it begins to color, add the blended tomatoes and the wine, thyme, sugar, Aleppo pepper, and some salt. Simmer, uncovered, for about 20 minutes, until the sauce is reduced and aromatic. Add the prawns and cook for 1 minute more, until they turn pink. Set this sauce aside.

Bring a large pan of water to a boil, add the fish stock cubes and some salt (not too much salt as the cubes are already salty) and stir to dissolve them. Add the spaghetti and cook until al dente, then drain.

Serve the pasta with the sauce poured over, drizzled with the extra-virgin olive oil, and sprinkled with the parsley.

PAN-FRIED FISH WITH GARLIC, VINEGAR, AND ALEPPO PEPPER

This simple fish dish is fabulous. In Spain, I would eat a whole fish, cooked open like a book, a la espalda, in the pan, with this dressing, but fillets will do very well. Use hake, bream, or sea bass, with the skin on. Serve with herby mashed potatoes with olive oil (page 123) or, for a quick pantry side, the white cannellini beans opposite. You can make it for more people by roasting the fillets in the oven (see Note).

Serves 2

2 hake, bream, or sea bass fillets, skin-on

salt

4 tbsp / 60ml extra-virgin olive oil

5 large garlic cloves, sliced

1 good pinch Aleppo pepper

2 to 3 tsp sherry vinegar or white wine vinegar

1 tbsp chopped flat-leaf parsley

Season the fish with salt. Warm 1 tbsp of the olive oil in a heavy nonstick skillet over medium-low heat. Add the fillets, skin-side down, and press with a spatula to flatten them as the skin curls. Cook until the skin is crisp and lightly browned. They will gradually cook through almost to the top. The timing depends on the type and thickness of the fish, and will take 2 to 5 minutes, but do not overcook – they are done when the flesh flakes when you cut into the thickest part with a knife. Turn and cook the flesh side for a few seconds more.

In a small pan over low heat, gently warm the remaining 3 tbsp olive oil with the garlic and Aleppo pepper until the garlic is only just lightly golden and crunchy (do not let it get brown). Take this dressing off the heat and stir in the vinegar, to taste.

Serve the fish very hot, with the dressing poured over, sprinkled with the parsley.

White cannellini beans

Warm 1 tbsp olive oil in a skillet over low heat. Fry a chopped onion, stirring, for 5 minutes, until soft and beginning to color. Drain a 15-oz / 425g can cannellini beans, rinse, then add to the onion. Season with salt and black pepper, add a few fresh thyme leaves and 7 tbsp / 100ml water, and cook, covered, for 5 minutes. Serve drizzled with 1 to 2 tbsp extra-virgin olive oil.

Note

If you want to serve more than two people, you can make this as a sheet-pan meal. Preheat the oven to 400°F. Lay the fish fillets skin-side down in an oiled sheet pan, brush them with olive oil, season with salt, and cook for 12 to 15 minutes. Make the dressing as directed, multiplying the rest of the ingredients.

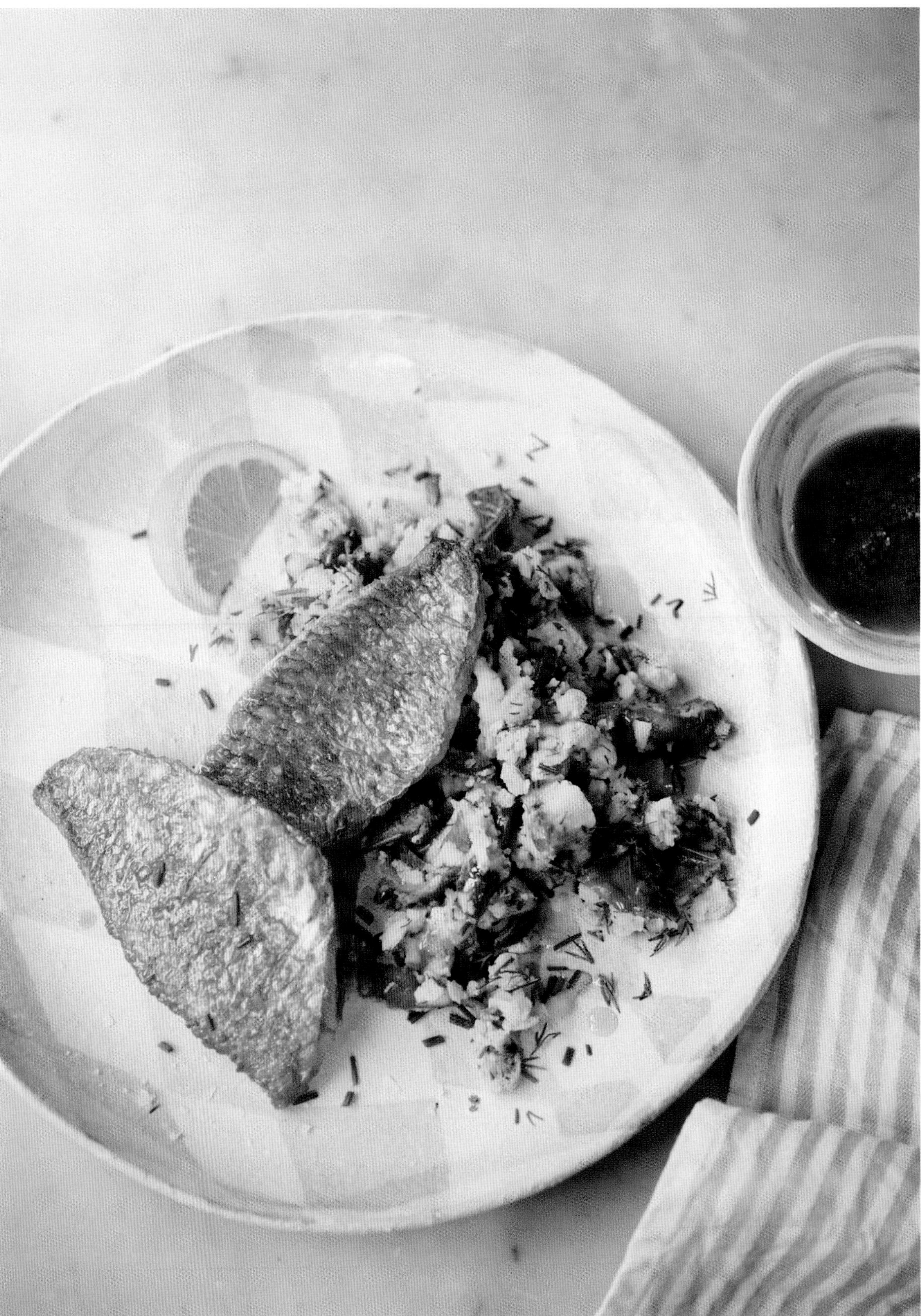

RED MULLET WITH PROVENÇAL MASHED POTATOES

Red mullet is often paired with black olives. They bring out its rosy tint and unique delicate flavor. There are olives and sun-dried tomatoes in these mashed potatoes, and sometimes I make an olivade (see below) to dab on the fish. The red mullet that I find at the fishmonger is usually in large fillets, not the small whole fish.

Serves 4

1 lb 10 oz / 740g baking potatoes, peeled

6 tbsp / 90ml extra-virgin olive oil, or a half-and-half mix of olive oil and sunflower oil

salt and black pepper

16 black olives, pitted and coarsely chopped

16 sun-dried tomatoes in oil, coarsely chopped

1 fresh red chile, finely chopped (optional)

1 good handful chopped herbs, such as parsley, chives, and dill

2 tbsp olive oil

4 large red mullet fillets, skin-on

Boil the potatoes in salted water until soft. Drain, keeping about ⅔ cup / 160ml of the cooking water. Mash the potatoes and beat in the extra-virgin olive oil or olive oil and sunflower oil. Season with salt and pepper and stir in just enough of the cooking water to give a soft, slightly moist mash. Then stir in the olives, tomatoes, chile (if using), and herbs and mix well.

Warm the 2 tbsp oil in a nonstick skillet over medium heat. Add the fillets, skin-side down, and cook for about 3 minutes, then turn them over and cook for 30 seconds, until cooked through.

Serve the fish with the mashed potatoes.

Olivade

For an olive paste to serve with the fish, blend ⅔ cup / 110g pitted black olives with a crushed garlic clove, 7 tbsp / 100ml extra-virgin olive oil, and 1 tbsp sherry vinegar.

FISH À LA PROVENÇALE IN TOMATO SAUCE

The enticing mingled aromas of ginger, saffron, orange and lemon peel, honey, and Aleppo pepper are of Provence. They make one of the most luscious sauces for fish I know. You can use any white fish such as monkfish, hake, or cod, and also salmon steaks or thick fillets. Use this sauce also with broiled, pan-fried, or roasted fish.

Serves 4

2¼ lb / 1kg ripe tomatoes, or two 14.5-oz / 411g cans whole tomatoes

5 tbsp / 75ml olive oil

4 garlic cloves, chopped

1 good pinch saffron threads

1 to 1¼ tsp ground ginger

grated zest of ½ orange

grated zest of ½ lemon

salt

1½ tbsp honey

1 good pinch Aleppo pepper

4 thick skinless fish fillets or steaks

black pepper

all-purpose flour for coating

¼ cup / 10g chopped flat-leaf parsley

12 good-quality black olives, pitted (optional)

1 tbsp capers, drained (optional)

If using fresh tomatoes, wash and quarter them, then remove the little white hard bits at the stem end. Blend the tomatoes to a creamy consistency in a food processor.

In a wide pan over low heat, warm 2 tbsp of the olive oil. Add the garlic and stir for less than 1 minute, until the aroma rises and it just begins to color. Add the blended tomatoes, saffron, ginger, citrus zests, and some salt. Stir well and simmer for about 10 minutes, until the tomatoes are reduced. Add the honey and Aleppo pepper and cook, stirring, for a few moments more.

Season the fish with salt and black pepper. Put a generous amount of flour on a plate and turn the fish fillets in this to coat them all over, then shake vigorously to remove excess flour.

Warm the remaining 3 tbsp oil in a nonstick skillet over medium heat. Add the fish and cook for 3 to 4 minutes (or up to 10 minutes), depending on the fish and the thickness of the fillets, turning them over once, until lightly browned and just cooked through. (If you make it with salmon, which I often use, it should be slightly underdone.)

Serve the fish on the sauce, sprinkled with the parsley and garnished, if you like, with the olives and capers.

Variation

For an intriguing anise flavor, add 3 tbsp pastis, raki, or ouzo to the sauce at the same time as the seasonings.

SALMON COOKED IN FOIL WITH SALSA VERDE

When we are at my daughter Anna's house, she often cooks a whole salmon. She serves it hot with boiled new potatoes and this refreshing Italian salsa verde. Hot or cold, it is the perfect lunch on a summer's day. Cooking the fish in foil keeps the flesh moist and juicy. It is beautiful – pale pink against the bright green salsa.

Ask the fishmonger to fillet and skin the fish and keep the head to use for presentation.

Serves 8 to 10

2 tbsp olive oil

1 whole salmon (about 5½ lb / 2.5kg), filleted and skinned

salt and black pepper

⅔ cup / 160ml dry white wine

Salsa verde

1 large bunch flat-leaf parsley, stems removed

⅔ cup / 80g pine nuts

5 small gherkins

8 pitted green olives

3 garlic cloves, crushed

3 tbsp wine vinegar, or the juice of ½ lemon

¾ to 1 cup / 175 to 240ml very mild extra-virgin olive oil

salt and black pepper

Preheat the oven to 400°F.

Lay a large sheet of heavy-duty double-width foil in a roasting pan (or double up two thinner sheets), brush with the olive oil, and place the two salmon fillets on it, one on top of the other. Season with salt and pepper. Bring the edges of the foil up over the fish to surround it and pour in the wine. Fold the foil edges together to make a sealed loose parcel (it should not be tight). Wrap the head in another piece of greased foil and put it in the roasting pan.

Place the roasting pan in the oven and cook for 30 to 40 minutes. Salmon is best a little underdone, so check after 30 minutes – open the foil parcel and cut into the thickest part of the fish with the point of a knife. The flesh should flake but still be translucent in the center. If serving cold, let the fish cool in the foil parcel.

For the salsa verde, put all the ingredients except the extra-virgin olive oil in a food processor, season with salt and pepper, and blend, gradually adding the oil to make a light paste.

Serve the salmon hot or cold; put the head in place at the top of the fish. Pass the salsa verde alongside.

LE BAR D

LA MARINE

FRIED FISH WITH CUMIN AND TAHINI SAUCE

I was sitting in a restaurant in Tripoli, Lebanon, overlooking the sea, eating fried fish. The crisp sea bream with a delicate lemony tahini sauce, the smell of the sea, the gentle breeze, and the brilliant light took me back to Xenophon, the Greek fish restaurant in Alexandria where we always stopped on our arrival from Cairo when I was a child. The joy of it! I wanted to cry.

Serve this with herby mashed potatoes with olive oil (page 123).

Serves 4

Tahini sauce

3 tbsp tahini (stirred in the jar)

juice of ½ to 1 lemon

2 to 3 tbsp water

salt

1 small garlic clove, crushed (optional)

4 firm, skinless white fish fillets, such as bream or sea bass

salt

3 tbsp all-purpose flour

1 to 1½ tsp ground cumin

2 tbsp olive oil

1 lemon, quartered

1 tbsp chopped flat-leaf parsley

For the tahini sauce, put the tahini in a small serving bowl. Gradually add the lemon juice and water, beating vigorously with a fork and adding just enough water to get the consistency of a runny cream. The paste will stiffen at first and then become light and smooth. Season with a little salt and stir in the garlic (if using). Set aside.

Season the fish with salt. Put the flour, cumin, and a pinch of salt on a plate and mix well. Turn the fish fillets in this to coat them all over, then shake vigorously to remove excess flour.

Warm the olive oil in a nonstick skillet over medium heat. Add the fillets and cook, turning them over once, for 3 to 10 minutes depending on their thickness, until crisp, lightly browned, and just cooked through (the flesh should be opaque when you gently cut in with a knife).

Serve the fish with the lemon quarters and sprinkled with the parsley. Pass the tahini sauce around for people to help themselves.

BRODETTO

A fish soup is immensely satisfying. Everyone is happy with this very simple Italian brodetto. You find versions of it all around the coasts of Italy. You need a firm-fleshed fish, ideally monkfish, but others will do too. When my grandson Cesar made it, his fishmonger suggested cod cheeks were good for a soup, and they were.

Serves 4

1⅔ cups / 395ml dry white wine

2½ cups / 590ml fish stock or water

12 oz / 340g new potatoes, peeled and sliced

9 oz / 255g tomatoes, peeled and cut in big pieces

4 garlic cloves, chopped

2 fresh red chiles (optional)

2 tsp sugar, or to taste

salt

1 lb / 450g skinless fish fillets, such as monkfish

bread for serving

Aleppo pepper for serving

Put the wine and stock or water in a large pan. Add the potatoes, tomatoes, garlic, and chiles (if using). Bring to a boil and simmer for 30 minutes, then add the sugar and season with salt. Remove the chiles when you feel the soup is spicy enough.

Just before serving, add the fish fillets and cook for 5 to 10 minutes, until they just begin to flake when you cut into them with a knife.

Serve the soup with bread, and pass Aleppo pepper around for people to serve themselves if they want to.

BULLINADA

The Catalan bullinada is like the bourride of the French Riviera and the gazpachuelo of Malaga – a fish soup with garlic mayonnaise stirred in. It has a mysterious, delicate flavor and beautiful warm color. It is sometimes made with tiny baby squid, or a mix of shrimp and shellfish. I make it with white fish alone for friends who cannot eat shellfish. Use hake, monkfish, or cod cheeks. You can make much of it in advance and finish the soup a few minutes before you are ready to eat.

Serves 6

2 tbsp olive oil

1 large onion, chopped

8 garlic cloves; 6 cloves finely chopped, 2 cloves crushed

1 good pinch saffron threads

2 qt / 1.9L fish stock

7 tbsp / 100ml dry white wine

1¾ lb / 800g new potatoes, peeled and cut into ½-inch slices

1 tsp fennel seeds

strips of peel from ½ orange

salt and black pepper

1¾ lb / 800g skinless fish fillets, such as hake or monkfish

¾ cup / 175ml good-quality mayonnaise

juice of ½ lemon

1 good pinch Aleppo pepper, plus more for serving

¼ cup / 10g chopped flat-leaf parsley

In a wide pan over low heat, warm the olive oil. Fry the onion, stirring occasionally, for 5 minutes, until it begins to soften. Add the chopped garlic and stir for 2 minutes, until it just begins to color.

Stir the saffron into the onion and pour in the fish stock and wine, then add the potatoes, fennel seeds, and orange peel and season with salt and black pepper. Simmer, covered, for 20 to 25 minutes, until the potatoes are tender.

About 10 minutes before you are ready to serve, remove the orange peel and add the fish. Cook, covered, over low heat for 4 to 10 minutes, depending on the fish and the thickness of the fillets, until the fish becomes opaque and the flesh begins to flake when you cut into it with a knife. Break the fillets into pieces.

In a liquid measuring cup, beat the mayonnaise with the lemon juice, crushed garlic, and Aleppo pepper.

Just before serving, add a ladleful or two of the hot stock into the mayonnaise mixture and beat it in, then gently stir into the simmering soup. Heat through but do not let it boil or the mayonnaise will curdle. Serve the bullinada sprinkled with the parsley, and pass some Aleppo pepper for anyone who would like to add more.

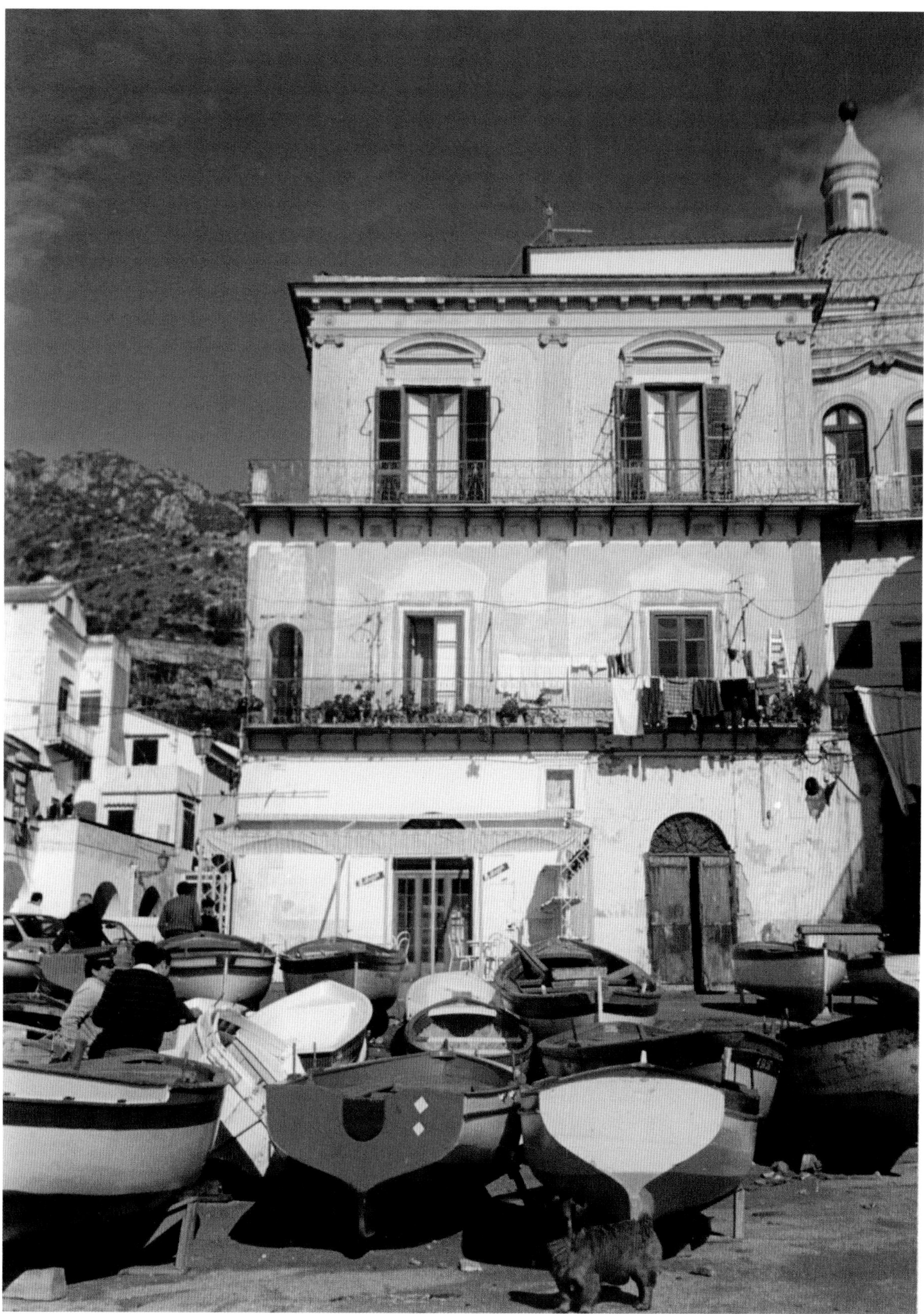

BOUILLABAISSE

Bouillabaisse belongs to the most colorful, bustling, cosmopolitan, multicultural port city of the Mediterranean – Marseille. Starting as a fisherman's way of using fish that have not sold, it became a trendy delicacy and something of an event. This easy, accessible bouillabaisse does not have the bony rascasse and other traditional fish, crustaceans, and shellfish you may find in Marseille, but it does have the magnificent flavors. Using good-quality fish stock means you can concentrate on the aromatics. You can make most of it in advance but you have to be ready to deal with two or three pans at the same time 15 minutes before serving. The optional clams and mussels are cooked separately; keep them in the fridge until you are ready to use them. Serve the soup with homemade aïoli or rouille (see pages 174 to 175) or an easy saffron aïoli (see opposite) spread on lightly toasted bread.

Serves 4 to 6

4 cups / 950ml good-quality fish stock

½ onion, chopped

½ fennel bulb with feathery leaves, chopped

1 large tomato

3 thyme sprigs, leaves only

2 bay leaves

1 tsp fennel seeds

grated zest of ½ orange

1 good pinch saffron threads

½ cup / 120ml dry white wine

1 tsp sugar, to taste

¼ cup / 60ml anise-flavored spirit such as pastis, arak, raki, or ouzo

1 lb / 450g waxy new potatoes

1 to 2¼ lb / 450g to 1kg clams or mussels (optional)

1 lb / 450g white fish fillets, such as monkfish or bream

5 oz / 140g raw peeled tiger prawns

1 large bunch flat-leaf parsley, leaves chopped

Warm the fish stock in a large pan over medium heat. Add the onion, fennel bulb, tomato, thyme, bay leaves, fennel seeds, orange zest, saffron, and wine and simmer for 30 to 45 minutes. Stir in the sugar, if you like, and anise-flavored spirit at the end.

Cook the potatoes in boiling salted water until tender, then drain. When cool enough to handle, peel – or not, as you like – and cut them into slices. Return them to the pan.

If using clams or mussels, wash them in plenty of cold water (pull off the "beards" from the mussels). Throw away any that are broken and any open ones that do not close when you tap them on the sink or dip them in ice-cold water. Scrub them with a brush if they are dirty, then leave in fresh cold water for 20 minutes – they will push out any sand that remains inside. Lift them out and rinse them in cold water.

About 15 minutes before you are ready to serve, reheat the stock. Add the fish and prawns and simmer until cooked through. Monkfish takes 10 to 15 minutes, so put it in first; the prawns take 2 minutes, so put them in last. Cut the fish into chunks.

At the same time, pour 1 to 2 tbsp of the fish stock over the potatoes and heat through with the lid on.

Put the clams or mussels in a pan with less than a finger of water, put the pan over high heat, and put the lid on. As soon as the bivalves open (within a minute or two), remove them from the heat – they are cooked. Throw away any that haven't opened.

Serve the bouillabaisse in soup bowls – potatoes at the bottom and fish on top, sprinkled with the parsley.

Lemony saffron aïoli

Beat ½ cup / 120ml good-quality mayonnaise with the juice of ½ lemon and one or two crushed garlic cloves. Warm a good pinch of saffron threads in 1 tbsp water and stir into the aïoli.

SICILIAN FISH CUSCUSU IMPERIALE OF TRAPANI

I was on the jury of a couscous competition in San Vito lo Capo, near Trapani in Sicily. There was always an annual local festa del couscous, then it went international and every country that has a couscous tradition was invited to participate. The streets were in a carnival mood with lights, musicians, cooking demonstrations, and tastings. The competition was carried out with pomp and ceremony. Each delegation marched with their couscous on a big tray and their flag, accompanied by their national anthem. The Italians won. Their fish cuscusu was sublime. It is the local dish in the little fishing village–turned–holiday resort of Trapani, where all kinds of seafood are used. Songs and poems are written about it and it features in legends and proverbs.

When I celebrated my eightieth birthday with the family in Sicily, I had a simpler version in a restaurant, which I've tried to reproduce. It is worth making for a lot of people and it's easy to double the quantities. As well as the grain and a stock in which you poach the seafood, there's the fresh tomato and almond pesto trapanese, which can be delicate and aromatic, but if you like it hot you can use plenty of Aleppo pepper; it can be made in advance and kept, covered, in the fridge.

Serves 4

3½ cups / 830ml good-quality fish stock

⅔ cup / 160ml dry white wine

1 good pinch saffron threads

1½ cups / 250g couscous

1 tbsp extra-virgin olive oil

Trapani pesto

14 oz / 400g ripe plum tomatoes

1 to 4 garlic cloves, crushed, to taste

1 tsp sugar

¾ tsp ground ginger

¼ cup / 60ml extra-virgin olive oil

1 very good pinch Aleppo pepper, or piment d'Espelette

salt

½ cup / 55g sliced almonds

1 bunch basil, leaves chopped

grated zest of ½ orange

10 oz / 285g skinless fish fillets, such as monkfish or hake

7 oz / 200g raw peeled king prawns

In a stockpot over medium heat, warm the fish stock with the wine and saffron. Put the couscous in a wide baking dish from which you can serve it and pour in 1½ cups / 360ml of the fish stock, stirring well so that it is absorbed evenly. Let sit for about 15 minutes, stirring again once or twice, until the grain has absorbed the liquid and is tender. Stir in the olive oil and rub the couscous between your hands above the dish to aerate the grains and break up any lumps.

For the Trapani pesto, cut the tomatoes into quarters and remove the little white hard bits at the stem end. Put in a food processor with the garlic, sugar, ginger, olive oil, Aleppo pepper or piment d'Espelette, and a little salt and blend to a creamy consistency. Add the almonds and basil and blend briefly until the almonds are very coarsely chopped.

Preheat the oven to 400°F. Cover the dish of couscous with foil. About 10 minutes before serving, put the couscous in the oven to reheat. Bring the remaining fish stock to a boil, taste and adjust the seasoning, and add the orange zest. Add the fish and simmer for 5 minutes, then add the prawns and cook for 1 to 2 minutes more, until they turn pink.

Pour the pesto all over the hot couscous and arrange the fish and prawns on top. Pour some broth over each serving.

MEAT AND POULTRY

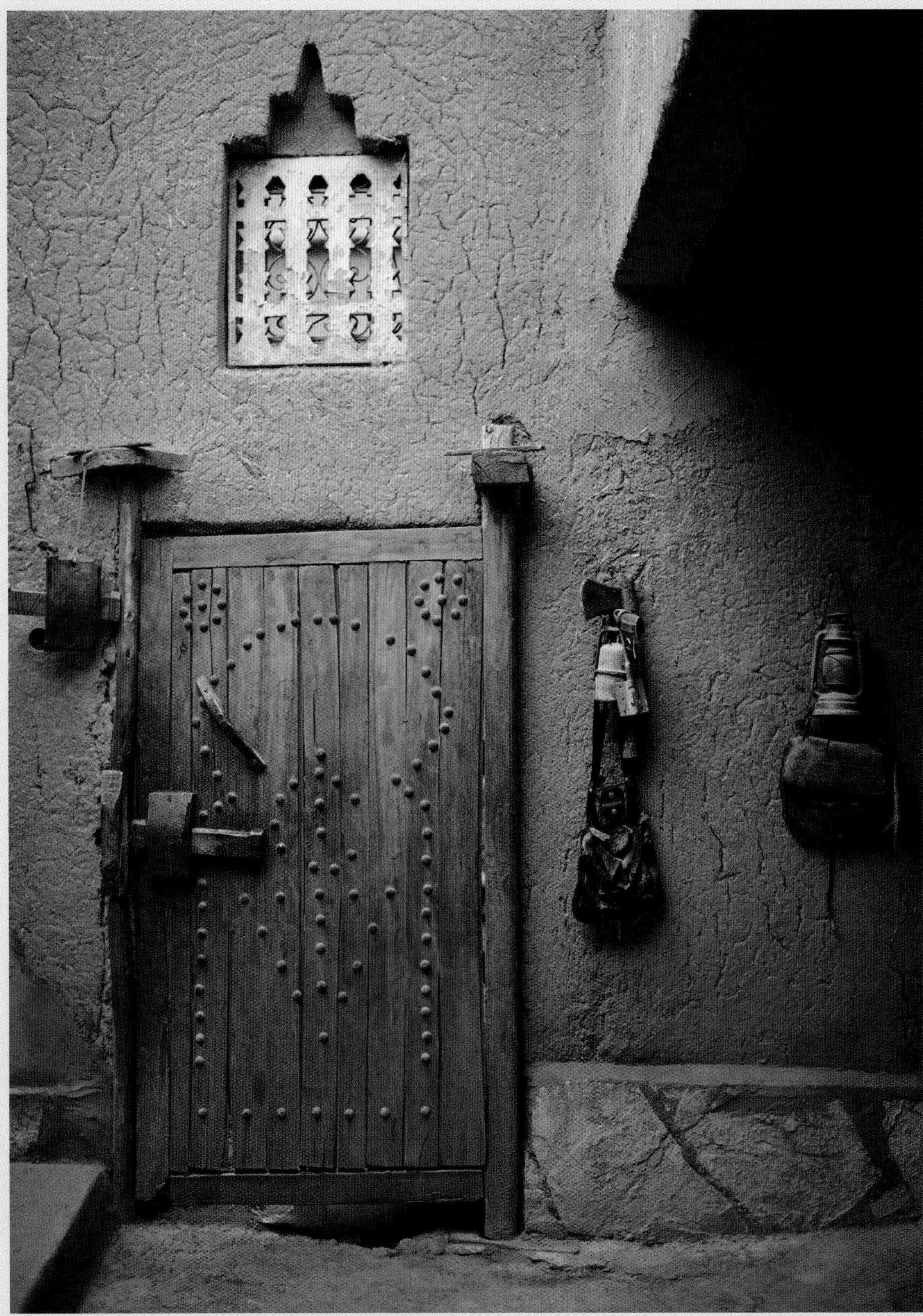

I could tell by the aromas wafting from behind the walls what spices were being used, and at what stage the cooking was. In the labyrinth of alleys in the medina, someone was roasting lamb, someone was frying fish, somewhere a tagine was beginning to sizzle and caramelize. I was in Fez to speak at a festival celebrating the regional cooking of Morocco, and one of the helpers had invited me to her home. I arrived at a tiny door in a windowless mud-colored wall. I thought it might lead into a hovel, but it opened into a paradise – a perfumed garden lined with cobalt and turquoise mosaics, with orange and lemon trees, a fig tree, vines, and jasmine. It was the courtyard of an old riad that had seen better days but was all the more glorious and moving for that. We sat on low sofas in an alcove and ate kemias (appetizers) while cone-shaped clay pots cooked gently on Primus stoves in the courtyard. When the tagine came, it was heaven. The sharpness of the fruit married with spices and a touch of honey to give the meltingly tender lamb a mysterious, delicate flavor.

Meat is the prestige food of the Mediterranean, and chicken is the popular everyday food. The area is sheep country and the usual meat is lamb and mutton. In Christian countries, the cooking of the mountain interior is dominated by pig. There is not enough humidity nor the right terrain for cattle raising – traditionally, beef is used in small quantities in fillings or stuffings. There are goats; ducks and geese are part of the scenery around marshlands and rivers; pigeons and rabbits are raised; hare, wild boar, and wild birds are hunted; the sea is the route of millions of migrating quails, whose arrival, tired, on the beaches is the gastronomic event of the season. I have many recipes for all of these, but I included here the most accessible meats and poultry because that is what we all want to cook.

Many of the recipes in this chapter are inspired by the eastern and southern Mediterranean. I love their celebratory dishes, their slow-roasted and long-braised lamb, their delicately spiced meats, and those cooked with fruit. The area was on the early spice route from the East. It was the transit area, and the middlemen, the intermediaries, succumbed to the attractions of their merchandise. Each country has its favorites and its own special spice mixes. I always head for the spice street in the souk or bazaar. If you have ever walked through a spice street, you can never forget the intoxicating effect of the mingled scents and the extraordinary displays of red, brown, and golden powders, the knotted roots, bits of bark and wood, shriveled pods, seeds, berries, translucent resins, and curious-looking plants, bulbs, buds, petals, and stigmas. I always used to bring home as much as I could from trips. Now that I buy spices in London, I imagine the spice shops in Marrakesh and Istanbul.

When you use spices and aromatics, my advice is to start with little and to add more if you wish, after you have tasted, and that includes chile.

CHICKEN BAKED WITH OLIVES AND BOILED LEMON

The enticing aromas of mingled garlic, turmeric, and ginger here are the same as those that waft over the food stalls every night in Place Djemaa el Fna, the great square in Marrakesh that during the day is taken over by Berber musicians, storytellers, comedians, fire-eaters, and snake charmers.

The sharp lemony flavors of one of the most famous Moroccan tagines work marvelously in this bake. It is very saucy and can be served with basic couscous (see page 226) or with mashed potatoes (see page 123). It is the kind of easy dish I make when I have many guests.

Serves 8

juice of 2 lemons

6 tbsp / 90ml olive oil

1½ tsp ground turmeric

1½ tsp ground ginger

1½ tbsp honey

1 cup / 240ml dry white wine

salt and black pepper

1 whole head of garlic, cloves chopped

16 chicken thighs, bone-in, skin-on

¾ cup / 120g capers in brine, drained

1¼ cups / 200g pitted green olives

1 large or 2 small unwaxed boiled lemons (see page 226), cut into pieces, discarding the seeds

1 bunch cilantro, leaves chopped

Preheat the oven to 350°F.

In a large bowl, combine the lemon juice, olive oil, turmeric, ginger, honey, and wine; season with salt and pepper; and beat well. Add the garlic and chicken, turning the pieces so that they are well coated.

Arrange the chicken thighs in a large roasting pan or baking dish in which they fit snugly, putting the capers, olives, and boiled lemon pieces in between, and pour the liquid contents of the bowl all over. Bake for 1 hour, until the chicken is well browned and cooked through.

Serve the chicken sprinkled with the chopped cilantro.

continued

Variation

Add frozen artichoke bottoms to the pan with the olives and capers. You can find them in Middle Eastern stores in bags of nine.

Boiled lemons

Put whole unwaxed lemons in a pan with water to cover. Put a smaller lid on top to keep them down as they float, and boil for about 30 minutes, until they are very soft when you press them. If you don't use them right away, drain and let cool. Pack them whole, pressing into a jar, and cover with olive oil or sunflower oil. They will last a few weeks in the fridge. You can use them cut into pieces or blended to a paste.

Basic couscous

Put 3 cups / 480g couscous into a large baking dish. Add ½ to 1 tsp salt to 3 cups / 720ml warm water and gradually pour this all over the couscous, stirring so that it will be absorbed evenly. Let swell for 10 minutes, stirring a couple of times, then mix in 2 tbsp olive oil and rub the couscous between your hands above the dish to aerate the grains and break up any lumps. Cover with foil and place in the oven below the chicken for the last 10 to 15 minutes of the cooking time.

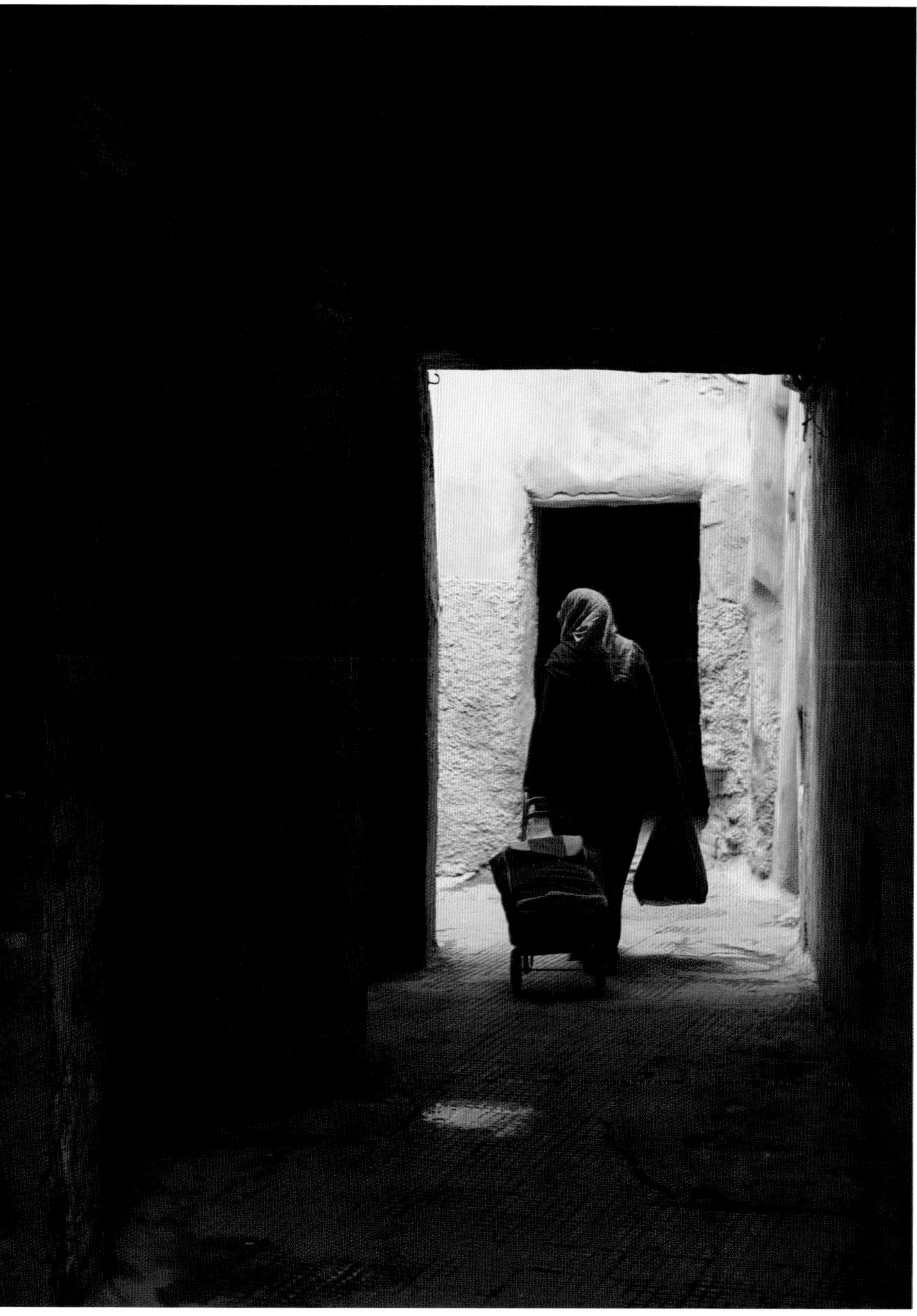

CHICKEN WITH GRAPES

When I asked people in Spain and in Italy what their favorite dishes were, several said chicken with grapes. I ate it in Tuscany with sweet wine and have made it many times that way, but in the end I prefer it without wine. Instead, the juices bursting out of the grapes come together with the chicken fat and juices to create a little sauce full of flavor.

This is lovely on a bed of polenta. Both chicken and polenta can be made in advance and heated through before serving. If you are making it in advance, pour the hot polenta into a large oiled sheet pan, smooth the top, and allow to cool. When you are ready to serve, cut it into four squares. Brush with sunflower oil or olive oil and toast under a hot broiler until very hot.

Serves 4

¼ cup / 60ml olive oil
2 rosemary sprigs, leaves only, chopped
8 chicken thighs, bone-in, skin-on
salt and black pepper
8 garlic cloves, peeled
1 lb / 450g seedless red grapes

Basic Polenta

3¾ cups / 890ml water
1 tsp salt
1⅓ cups / 185g instant polenta
5 tsp butter
black pepper

Warm the olive oil in a large sauté pan (wide enough to hold the chicken pieces in one layer) over medium heat. Add the rosemary and then the chicken, skin-side down. Season with salt and pepper and cook, covered, until the skin is browned and has released some of its fat. Turn the chicken pieces over, season again, and cook until the other side is browned.

Add the garlic and grapes to the pan. Put a lid on and cook over low heat for about 25 minutes, until the chicken is very tender and cooked through, turning the pieces over at least once. The grapes should be very soft; some will burst and their juice mixed with the chicken fat will make a rich, delicious sauce. Taste and check the seasoning – you need salt and pepper to balance the sweetness of the grapes.

For the polenta, meanwhile, in a large saucepan, bring the water to a boil and stir in the salt. Add the polenta in a thin stream, whisking vigorously. When it comes back to a boil (it will gurgle and splatter), turn the heat to very low and continue to stir for 2 minutes, until it is very thick. Cover the pan and cook for another 8 minutes, then stir in the butter and season with pepper.

Spoon the polenta into a shallow platter and top with the chicken and grapes. Serve hot.

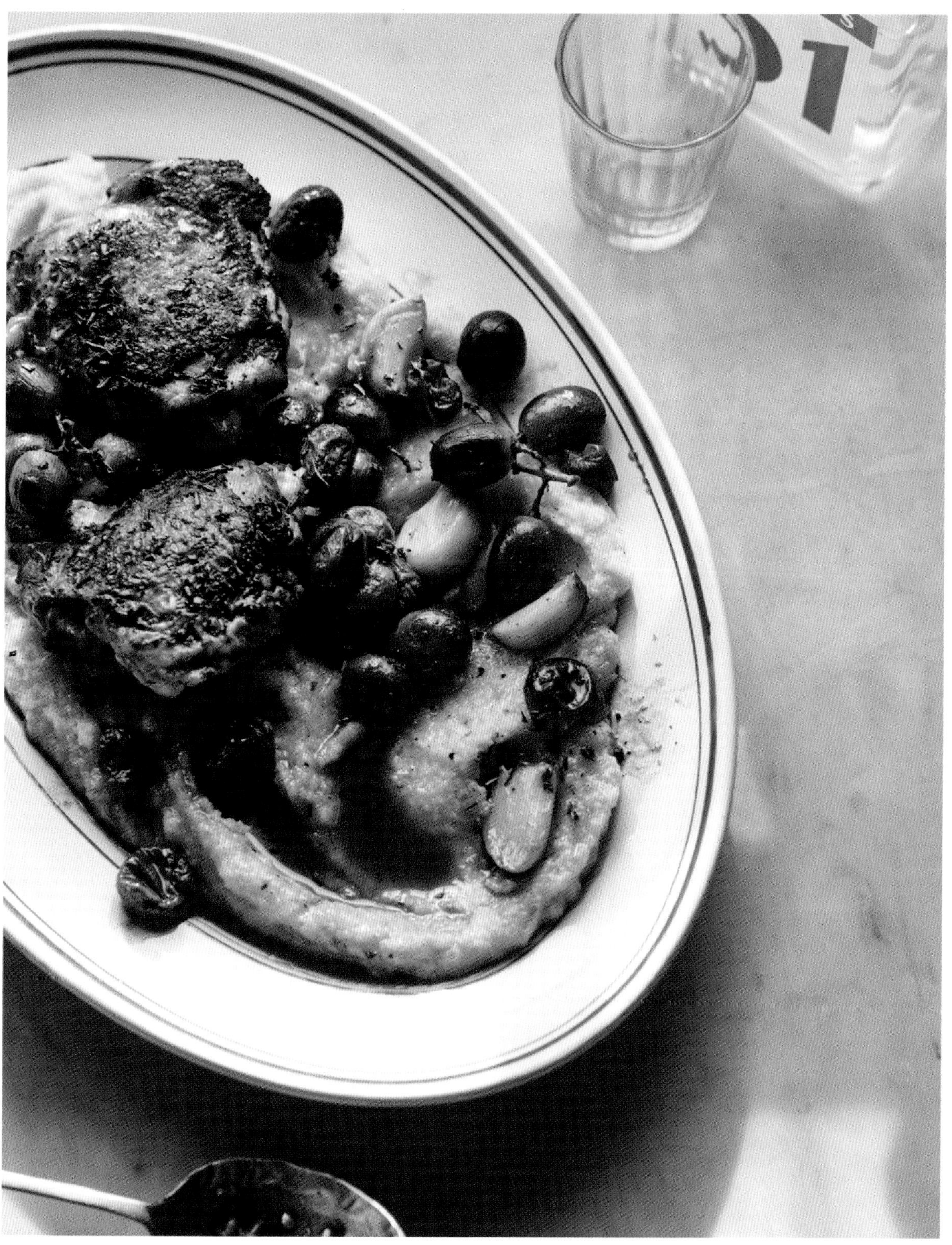

CHICKEN WITH WHITE WINE AND ROSEMARY

This is Italian and so simple. I was still working on this book in March 2020 and was retesting my recipes throughout lockdown while I was self-isolating. I kept ordering ingredients online and cooking and longing for someone to eat with me. Once, when my granddaughter Ruby arrived unexpectedly, I had just two chicken legs in the fridge and some fruity wine left in a bottle, so I made this. We sat in the garden at two separate tables. She loved it and asked me to put it in the book.

You can serve this with mashed potatoes (see page 123), mashed celery root, or polenta (see page 228).

Serves 2

2 tbsp butter
1 tbsp extra-virgin olive oil
2 chicken legs, bone-in, skin-on
salt and black pepper
¾ cup / 175ml dry white wine
2 garlic cloves, cut in half
2 rosemary sprigs
½ tsp sugar

Warm the butter and olive oil in a sauté pan or skillet over medium heat. Add the chicken legs and cook, turning the pieces to brown them all over.

Season the chicken with salt and pepper. Add the wine, garlic, rosemary, and sugar, then cover and simmer for 30 minutes, until the chicken is very tender and cooked through.

Serve the chicken hot.

CHICKEN WRAP INSPIRED BY THE FLAVORS OF PALESTINIAN MUSAKHAN

I ate this famously sharp and spicy Palestinian chicken dish on flatbreads in Jerusalem and loved it. I made it for my granddaughters Sarah, Ruby, and Nelly when we sat in the garden one night, and served it as tortilla wraps. They loved it, too, and enjoyed eating it in the wraps; they and their friends often eat like that. Serve with Greek yogurt and cucumber and tomato salad (page 84).

Serves 6

6 tbsp / 90ml sunflower oil or olive oil

3 large onions, halved and thickly sliced

3 to 4 tsp sumac, or more to taste

2 tsp ground cinnamon

1 tsp ground allspice

salt and black pepper

1 tsp ground cardamom, or 10 cardamom pods, cracked

8 boneless skinless chicken thighs

6 large flour tortillas

3½ oz / 100g pine nuts or sliced almonds, lightly toasted

Warm 2 tbsp of the oil in a large skillet or sauté pan over low heat. Sauté the onions with the lid on, stirring often and adding 1 tsp of the sumac, 1 tsp of the cinnamon, and ½ tsp of the allspice. Season with salt and pepper and cook for 45 minutes. The onions should be gently caramelized by then. If they are not, remove the lid and turn up the heat to medium for a minute or so.

In another large skillet or sauté pan, warm the remaining 4 tbsp / 60ml sunflower oil and stir in the remaining 2 to 3 tsp sumac, 1 tsp cinnamon, ½ tsp allspice, and the cardamom. Open the chicken thighs and put them in the pan, turning them in the spiced oil to coat all over. Add some salt and pepper, then cook over low heat, with the lid on, turning the chicken pieces over at least once, for 15 to 20 minutes, until tender and cooked through.

Cut the chicken into bite-size pieces and mix with the onions.

Heat the tortillas as instructed on the package. Put a tortilla on each plate. Spread some of the chicken-onion filling on one half and sprinkle with the pine nuts or sliced almonds. Let everyone roll or simply fold their own wraps.

CHICKEN AND ONION "PIES" WITH MOROCCAN FLAVORS

I have often enjoyed the Moroccan festive jewel-in-the-crown b'stilla, a pigeon pie, and have made it many times myself, with chicken encased in layers of paper-thin warka (pancakes) or more often with phyllo pastry. Here, I have drawn from the flavors of versions from Fez (famously sweet) and Tetouan (famously sharp and lemony). A light rectangle of puff pastry sits in for the crust. It is both sumptuous and easy.

Serves 4

14-oz / 400g all-butter puff pastry sheet

1 egg yolk mixed with a drop of water

2 large onions, halved and thickly sliced

¼ cup / 60ml olive oil or sunflower oil

¾ tsp ground ginger

1½ tsp ground cinnamon, plus more for sprinkling

generous ⅓ cup / 50g blanched almonds, coarsely chopped

6 boneless skinless chicken thighs, cut into bite-size pieces

salt and black pepper

1 to 2 tbsp lemon juice

grated zest of ½ orange

½ boiled lemon (see page 226), chopped (optional)

confectioners' sugar for dusting

1 bunch cilantro, leaves chopped

Preheat the oven to 400°F. Take the pastry out of the fridge about 20 minutes before you want to use it.

Place the pastry onto a lightly floured surface and roll out to a 15 x 11-inch rectangle Cut in half lengthwise, then cut each crosswise into four rectangles. Brush the tops with the egg yolk glaze and bake for 15 to 20 minutes, until the pastry has puffed up and is golden brown. Let cool.

Put the onions in a large skillet, add the oil, put the lid on, and cook over low heat, stirring often, for 10 to 12 minutes, until they are very soft.

Stir the ginger and cinnamon into the onions, then add the almonds and chicken pieces and season with salt and pepper. Cook, uncovered, for 7 to 8 minutes, stirring and turning the chicken until it is tender and lightly browned. Stir in the lemon juice, orange zest, boiled lemon (if using), and 3 to 4 tbsp water and continue to cook for 5 minutes.

Lightly cover the pastry rectangles with confectioners' sugar and a sprinkling of cinnamon.

Stir the cilantro into the chicken mixture and serve hot, with two pastry rectangles on the side of each plate.

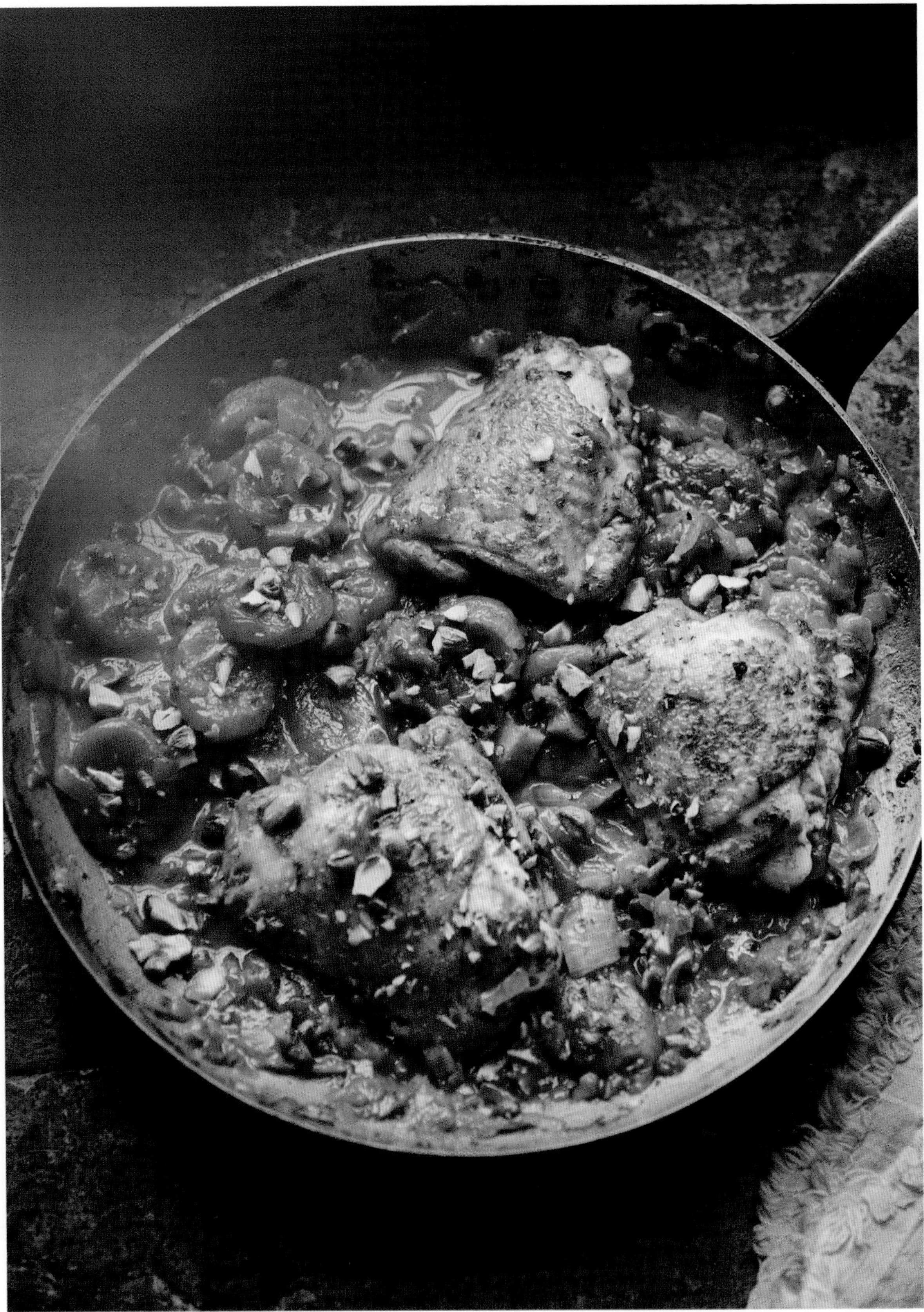

CHICKEN WITH APRICOTS AND PISTACHIOS

Meat with fruit is a legacy of ancient Persia that spread through the Arab world. When Teuntje Klinkenberg, a friend in the Netherlands, asked me for a medieval Persian recipe with chicken for the National Museum of Ceramics, I looked in a translation of a thirteenth-century Arab culinary manual. I was intrigued by a dish of chicken with apricots and pistachios, a combination familiar to my family and trending with chefs today. I invited my brother Ellis and sister-in-law Gill, who live nearby, to eat my modern interpretation. It was fascinating to find that the flavors of the past are still with us. Serve it with spiced saffron rice (page 153).

Serves 4

2 tbsp sunflower oil

2 onions, chopped

8 chicken thighs, bone-in, skin-on

salt and black pepper

7 oz / 200g soft dried apricots

1 tsp ground cinnamon

1 tsp ground coriander

1 tbsp pomegranate molasses

juice of ½ lemon

generous ½ cup / 75g pistachios, coarsely chopped

Warm the sunflower oil in a large sauté pan over low heat. Add the onions and cook, with the lid on, stirring often, for about 10 minutes, until soft and golden. Remove the onions and set them aside.

Put the chicken thighs into the pan, skin-side down, add salt and pepper, and cook over medium heat, with the lid on, for about 10 minutes, until the skin releases its fat and the chicken pieces are well browned. Turn them over and cook the other side for 10 minutes, until browned, adding more salt and pepper.

Add the apricots and return the onions to the pan, lifting the chicken pieces so that they sit on top of the apricots and onions.

Measure ¾ cup / 175ml water into a liquid measuring cup, stir in the cinnamon, coriander, pomegranate molasses, and lemon juice and pour over the chicken. Cook, covered, over low heat for 25 minutes, until the chicken is very tender and cooked through and the liquid is reduced.

Serve the chicken sprinkled with the pistachios.

CHICKEN WITH FREEKEH

The inspiration for this dish is my favorite Egyptian food: stuffed pigeon with freekeh, called *ferik* in Egypt. Freekeh is young green durum wheat that is harvested while still unripe and then roasted in a pile in the open. The straw and chaff burn and the moist grain acquires a smoky flavor. It is then rubbed to remove the chaff. There are two commercial varieties: the whole grain and the most commonly sold cracked freekeh that cooks more quickly.

Egyptian pigeons are not at all like the British bird, with their dark meat and gamey flavor – they are more like French pigeonneaux or squabs. I use chicken instead of pigeon with freekeh. Do try my interpretation – it is wonderful and very easy.

In 1988, I was in Cairo to write about pigeons. Raising them is one of the great passions of Egypt. People raise them as carrier and racing pigeons, and for eating when they are tiny. I saw pigeons peeking out of small mud-brick dovecotes on rooftops and balconies and hanging out of windows. When I lived there, Cairo was like two cities with their backs to each other. The part I lived in was built by French and Italian architects; the other, with meandering streets and bazaars, mosques, and mausoleums, was an old medieval Arab city. Rural Egypt was like an entirely different country, one that was centuries old. Now the entire city seemed swamped by the countryside. Millions of people had flooded in. There were flocks of sheep in the street, and chickens on the rooftops. I went to the souk el hammam, the pigeon market near the Citadel where hundreds of young boys and old men gather on Fridays to sell and exchange live birds. Some sat behind crates full of birds raised in farms outside the city, others stood holding only one or two. A few were selling very tiny baby ones for eating. Whenever it was on the menu, I ordered stuffed pigeon. The stuffing varied; sometimes rice was used, with almonds or pine nuts.

Serves 6

3 to 4 tbsp olive oil or sunflower oil
2 large onions, halved and sliced
1 tsp ground cinnamon
¼ tsp ground allspice
½ tsp ground cardamom
6 boneless skinless chicken thighs
salt and black pepper
juice of ½ to 1 lemon

Freekeh

1⅓ cups / 250g cracked freekeh
3 cups / 720ml chicken stock
½ tsp ground cinnamon
¼ tsp ground allspice
¼ tsp ground cardamom
¼ cup / 35g raisins
salt and black pepper
3 tbsp sunflower oil, or 2 tbsp butter

3½ oz / 100g pine nuts, lightly toasted
1 tbsp sumac
1⅔ cups / 400g Greek yogurt mixed with the juice of ½ lemon and a little salt

Warm the oil in a large skillet or sauté pan over low heat. Fry the onions with the lid on, stirring occasionally, for about 5 minutes, until they begin to soften. Stir in the cinnamon, allspice, and cardamom and add the chicken. Cook with the lid on, turning the chicken pieces a few times, stirring and seasoning with salt and pepper, for about 30 minutes, until the chicken is browned all over, very tender, and cooked through, and the onions are very soft and browned. Cut each thigh into smaller pieces, add the lemon juice to taste, and mix well.

For the freekeh, while the chicken is cooking, wash the freekeh in plenty of water in a bowl. Pour off any chaff or burnt grains that float to the top, then drain.

Put the chicken stock in a large pan with the cinnamon, allspice, and cardamom and bring to a boil. Add the freekeh and raisins, season with salt and pepper, and stir well. Simmer over low heat with the lid on for about 20 minutes, until the grain is very tender and the liquid has been absorbed. If there is too much liquid left, remove the lid and let it evaporate. Stir in the sunflower oil or butter.

Serve the freekeh hot, with the chicken and onions on top, sprinkled with the pine nuts and sumac and accompanied by the yogurt.

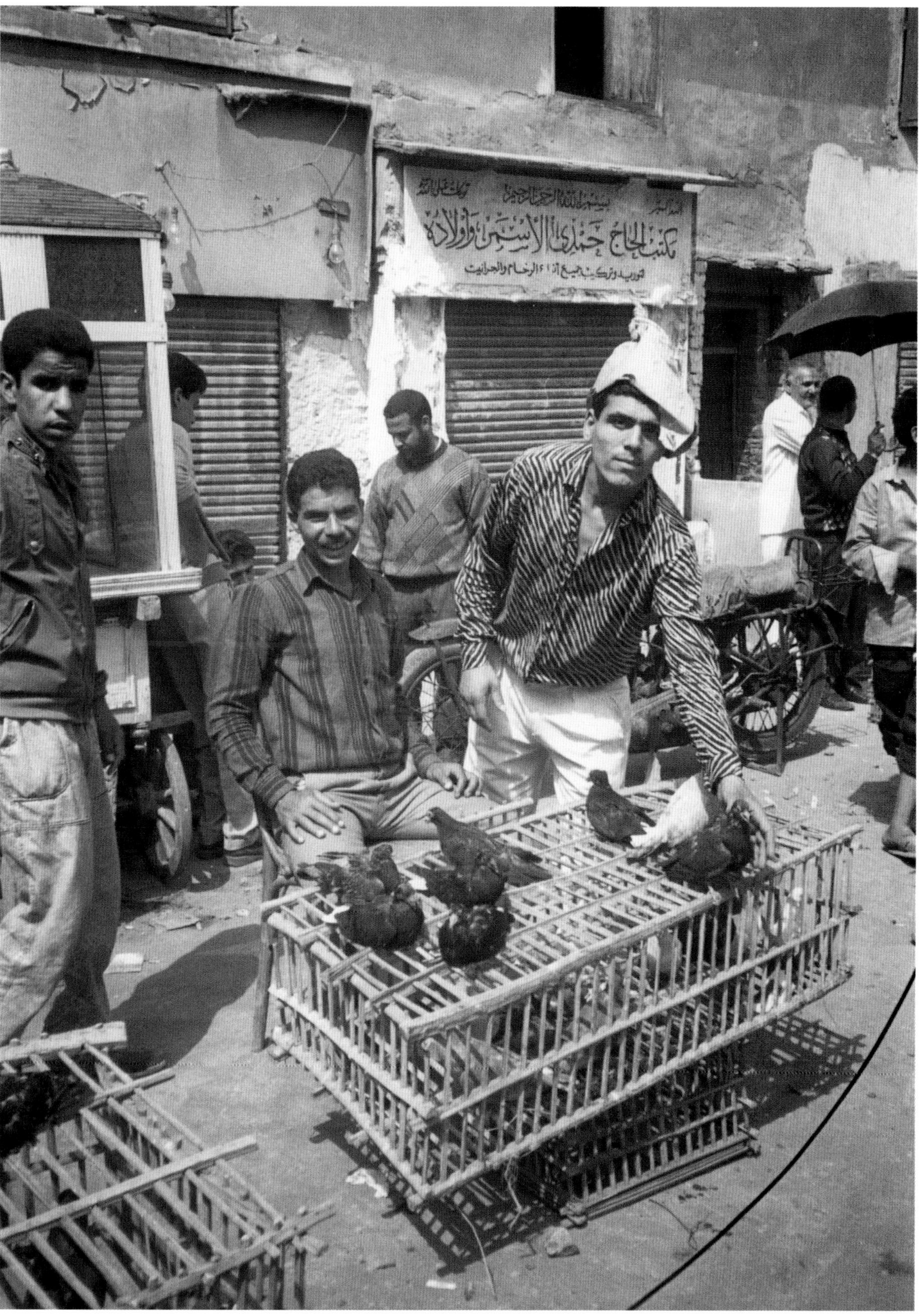
بسم الله الرحمن الرحيم
مكتب الحاج حمدى الأسمر وأولاده
توريد وتركيب جميع أنواع الرخام والجرانيت

CHICKEN IN A SPICY HONEY SAUCE BURIED IN VERMICELLI

We sat around a mountain of vermicelli decorated with chopped almonds and lines of cinnamon and confectioners' sugar. Everyone helped themselves, digging in to find pieces of ever-so-tender baby pigeon in a rich aromatic sauce. From my memories of this stunning dish, I've come up with a modest interpretation of shaariya medfouna (it means "buried in vermicelli"), a grand ceremonial dish of Fez. The savory-sweet sauce is a legacy of the Moors banished from Spain, who settled in this most Andalusian of North African cities.

You can cook the chicken in its sauce in advance and heat it through when you cook the vermicelli just before serving. I make this in a wide double-handled pan that I bring to the table. You need short fine egg noodles for this dish or fine dry vermicelli nests (not rice vermicelli); they are sometimes sold as capelli d'angelo or angel hair pasta.

Serves 4 to 6

¼ cup / 60ml olive oil

3 large onions, halved and sliced

2 tsp ground cinnamon

¾ tsp ground ginger

1 good pinch saffron threads

salt and black pepper

8 boneless skinless chicken thighs

1 cup / 240ml water

1½ tbsp aromatic honey

1 tbsp orange blossom water (optional)

1 good pinch Aleppo pepper (optional)

1 bunch cilantro or flat-leaf parsley, chopped

10 oz / 285g short fine egg noodles or dried vermicelli nests, crushed

3 tbsp butter

½ cup / 50g sliced almonds, lightly toasted

1 tsp confectioners' sugar (optional)

In a heavy-bottomed sauté pan (wide enough to hold the chicken thighs in one layer), warm the olive oil over low heat. Sauté the onions, with the lid on but stirring often, for about 10 minutes, until they begin to soften.

Add 1½ tsp of the cinnamon, the ginger, and saffron to the onions; season with salt and pepper; and stir well. Add the chicken and cook, covered, over low heat for about 8 minutes, stirring and turning the pieces of chicken over once.

Add the water and continue to cook, covered, over low heat for about 30 minutes, until the chicken is very tender and cooked through and the onions are meltingly soft.

Cut the thighs in half. Stir in the honey and orange blossom water (if using) and cook, uncovered, until the sauce is reduced and thickened, adding a little more water if it is too dry. Taste and adjust the seasoning; you need plenty of black pepper or the Aleppo pepper to mitigate the sweetness. Mix in the cilantro or parsley.

When you are ready to serve, cook the noodles in boiling salted water for 2 to 3 minutes, until al dente. Drain and return to the pan, stir in the butter, and season with salt, if necessary. Spread the noodles all over the chicken and garnish with the sliced almonds, remaining ½ tsp cinnamon, and, if you like, confectioners' sugar.

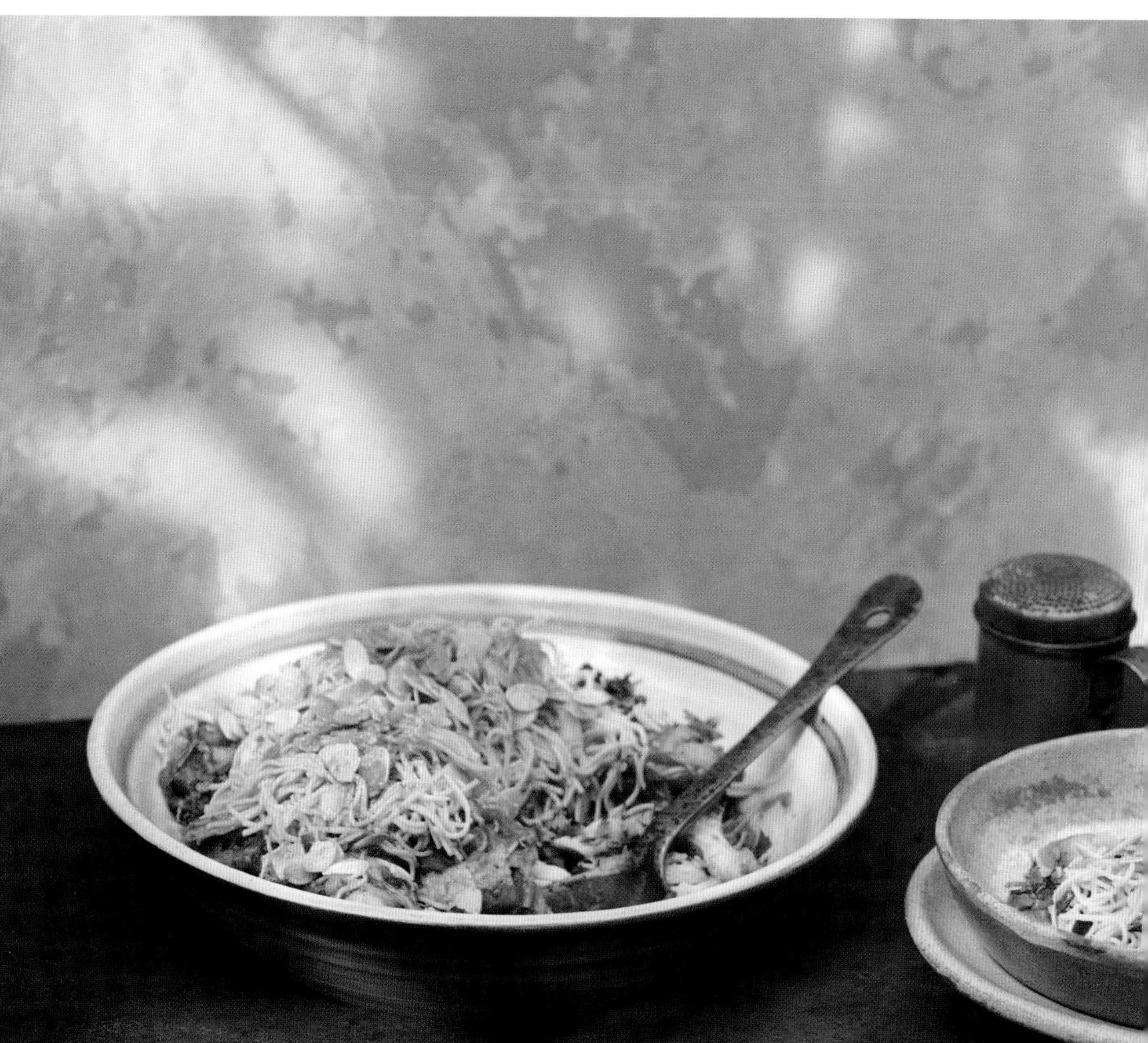

ROAST CHICKEN WITH BULGUR, RAISINS, CHESTNUTS, AND PINE NUTS

When my grandchildren were small, I made regular weekly meals for all the family and it was always roast chicken. It was what the grandchildren wanted and it was easy to put three chickens in the oven together. Bulgur – whole wheat kernels that have been boiled, then dried and ground – is a rural staple in Turkey and the Arab world. You often see it drying on rooftops in the countryside there. With chestnuts, raisins, pine nuts, and delicate spices, it makes a sophisticated accompaniment to the chicken.

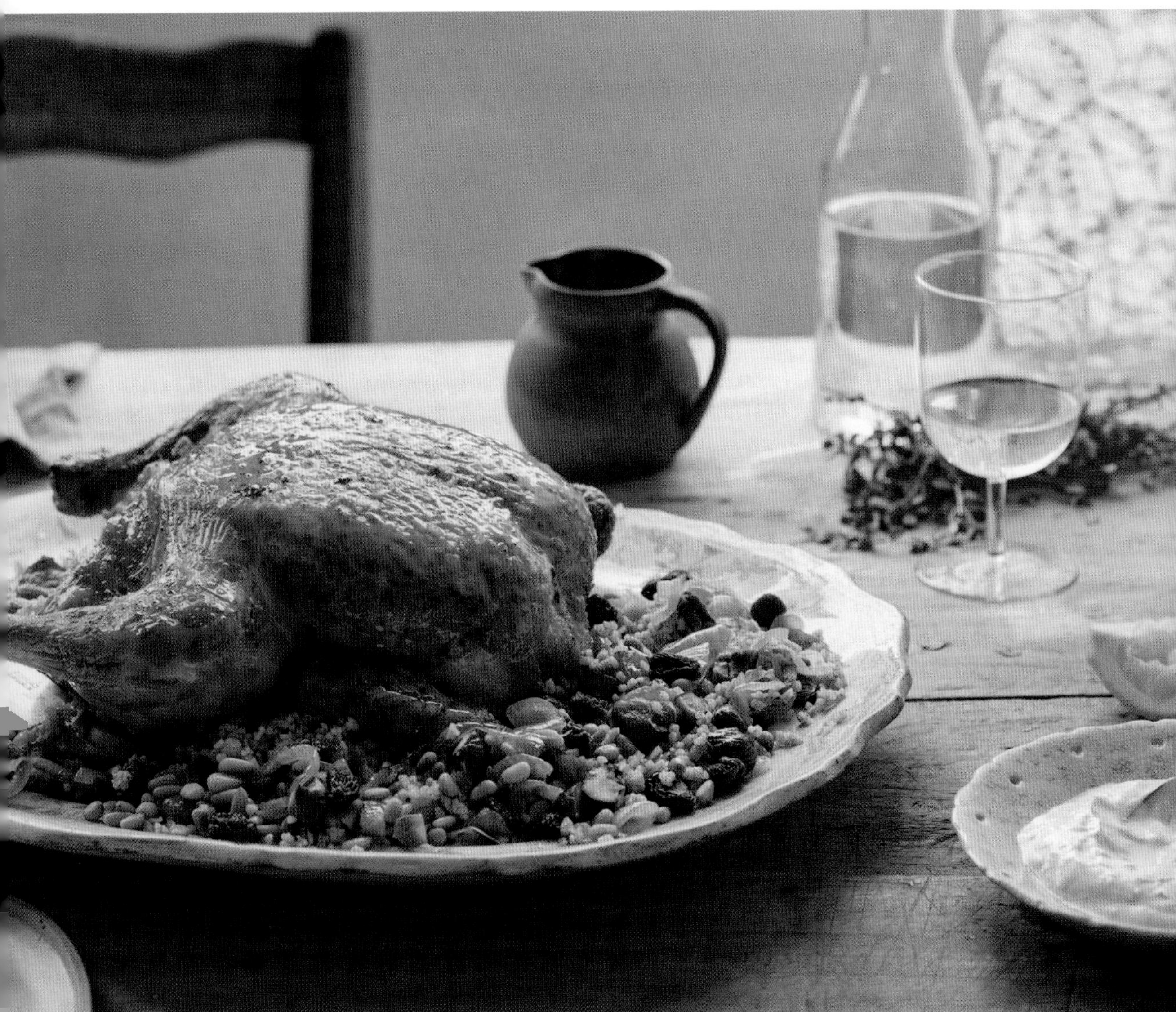

Serves 4 to 6

one 3½- to 4-lb / 1.6 to 1.8kg chicken

2 tbsp olive oil or sunflower oil

juice of ½ lemon

salt and black pepper

5 tbsp / 75ml water

Bulgur pilaf

2 tbsp olive oil or sunflower oil

1 large onion, halved and sliced

2 cups / 480ml chicken stock

1½ tsp ground cinnamon

½ tsp ground allspice

½ tsp ground coriander

salt

1½ cups / 250g bulgur

6 tbsp / 50g raisins, soaked in water for 15 minutes

3 tbsp butter, cut into pieces

black pepper

7 tbsp / 50g pine nuts

3½ oz / 100g cooked whole chestnuts, halved

Yogurt sauce

generous ¾ cup / 200g Greek yogurt

grated zest and juice of ½ lemon

grated zest of ½ orange

1 garlic clove, crushed (optional)

Preheat the oven to 400°F.

Rub the chicken with the oil and lemon juice, season with salt and pepper, and push the squeezed half lemon inside the cavity. Lay the chicken, breast-side down, in a baking dish and pour in the water. Roast for 1 hour, then turn the chicken breast-side up and roast for another 15 to 20 minutes, until the skin is crisp and brown and the juices run clear when you cut into the bird between the leg and the body with a knife.

For the bulgur pilaf, while the chicken is in the oven, warm the oil in a large skillet over medium heat. Fry the onion, with the lid on, for about 20 minutes, until browned and caramelized. Stir often and remove the lid toward the end.

At the same time, bring the chicken stock to a boil in a large pan. Stir in the cinnamon, allspice, coriander, and some salt (taking into consideration the saltiness of the stock). Stir in the bulgur and raisins and cook over low heat, with the lid on, for about 10 minutes, until the liquid has been absorbed and the grain is tender. Fold in the butter and add some pepper and more salt to taste.

Add the pine nuts and chestnuts to the skillet with the fried onions and cook, stirring, for 2 to 3 minutes, then mix into the bulgur.

For the yogurt sauce, beat together the yogurt, lemon zest and juice, orange zest, and garlic (if using) with a fork.

Cut the chicken into pieces and pour the lemony sauce that has formed in the baking dish over the chicken and bulgur. Serve with the yogurt sauce.

ROAST DUCK LEGS WITH PEACHES

The legs are the most tender and juicy part of a duck. Rubbed with sweet spices, with a touch of honey melting on them at the end of roasting, and partnered with ripe peaches, they are sumptuous. You can find duck legs in most supermarkets. Check the roasting times suggested by the producer, as they depend on how fat the duck is. Serve them with potatoes roasted in the duck fat.

Serves 4

4 duck legs

2 tbsp olive oil

¾ tsp ground ginger

¾ tsp ground cinnamon

salt and black pepper

4 ripe peaches, cut in half and pits removed

½ cup / 120ml sweet Malaga wine or other sweet wine

2 tbsp aromatic honey, such as orange blossom or acacia

Preheat the oven to 350°F.

Put the duck legs in a large baking dish, skin-side up, and prick them all over with a knife to let the fat from under the skin run out while cooking.

In a little bowl, mix the olive oil with the ginger and cinnamon and plenty of salt and black pepper, and rub some of this on each of the duck legs.

Roast the legs for 50 minutes.

Take the dish out of the oven, lift out the duck legs, and pour out some of the fat (pour it over potatoes – see Note). Return the duck legs to the dish, skin-side up, and put in the peaches, cut-sides up. Pour the wine over the peaches. Return to the oven and continue to cook for about 35 minutes.

Take the dish out of the oven, pour ½ tbsp honey over each leg, and return to the oven for 5 minutes – until the peaches are soft, the duck skin is crisp, and the meat is extremely soft and comes away from the bone easily – before serving.

Variation

Instead of peaches, use apricots – their sharpness cuts the richness of the duck meat.

Note

Have four potatoes ready (Yukon gold is a good choice). Peel them, cut into large pieces, and boil them in salted water for 10 minutes, then drain and shake in a colander to roughen their surfaces and turn out onto a sheet pan. Pour on the hot duck fat and turn the pieces to coat them all over (add a little olive oil if there is not enough fat). Season with salt and put them in the oven to roast with the duck legs for the last 40 minutes of the cooking time, turning them over once.

MEAT PIES IN PHYLLO PASTRY

When it comes to pies and wrapped foods, small is beautiful in the Arab world. For years, I made tiny meat cigars and triangles. They were delightful finger food but labor-intensive and not what I want to spend time on today. I devised this pastry envelope with the flavors of Aleppo as a fun snack or light main dish to serve with a salad or together with a mixed vegetable dish. You need a sturdy type of phyllo pastry that does not tear easily (look for phyllo labeled "country-style," "thick," or "horiatiko"). If your phyllo is very thin, you will need two layers with oil brushed between them for each parcel.

Serves 6

3 sheets thick (14 x 18-inch) phyllo dough

2 tbsp olive oil or sunflower oil, plus more for brushing

1 large onion, chopped

1 lb / 450g lean ground beef

¾ tsp salt

½ tsp black pepper

1 tsp ground cinnamon

½ tsp ground allspice

½ tsp ground ginger

2 tbsp pomegranate molasses

7 tbsp / 50g pine nuts, lightly toasted

1 large bunch flat-leaf parsley, leaves chopped

1 egg yolk mixed with a drop of water

2 tbsp sesame seeds or nigella seeds

Take the phyllo out of the fridge 30 minutes before you want to use it.

Warm the oil in a medium skillet over medium-low heat. Fry the onion for about 10 minutes, until golden. Add the beef, salt, pepper, cinnamon, allspice, and ginger and cook, breaking up the meat, crushing and turning it over until browned, for 8 to 10 minutes, adding the pomegranate molasses when the meat has begun to brown. Stir in the pine nuts and parsley and let cool.

Preheat the oven to 350°F.

Divide the meat filling into six portions. Open out the phyllo sheets and cut in half lengthwise. Keep them in a pile, covered with a tea towel so that they don't dry out.

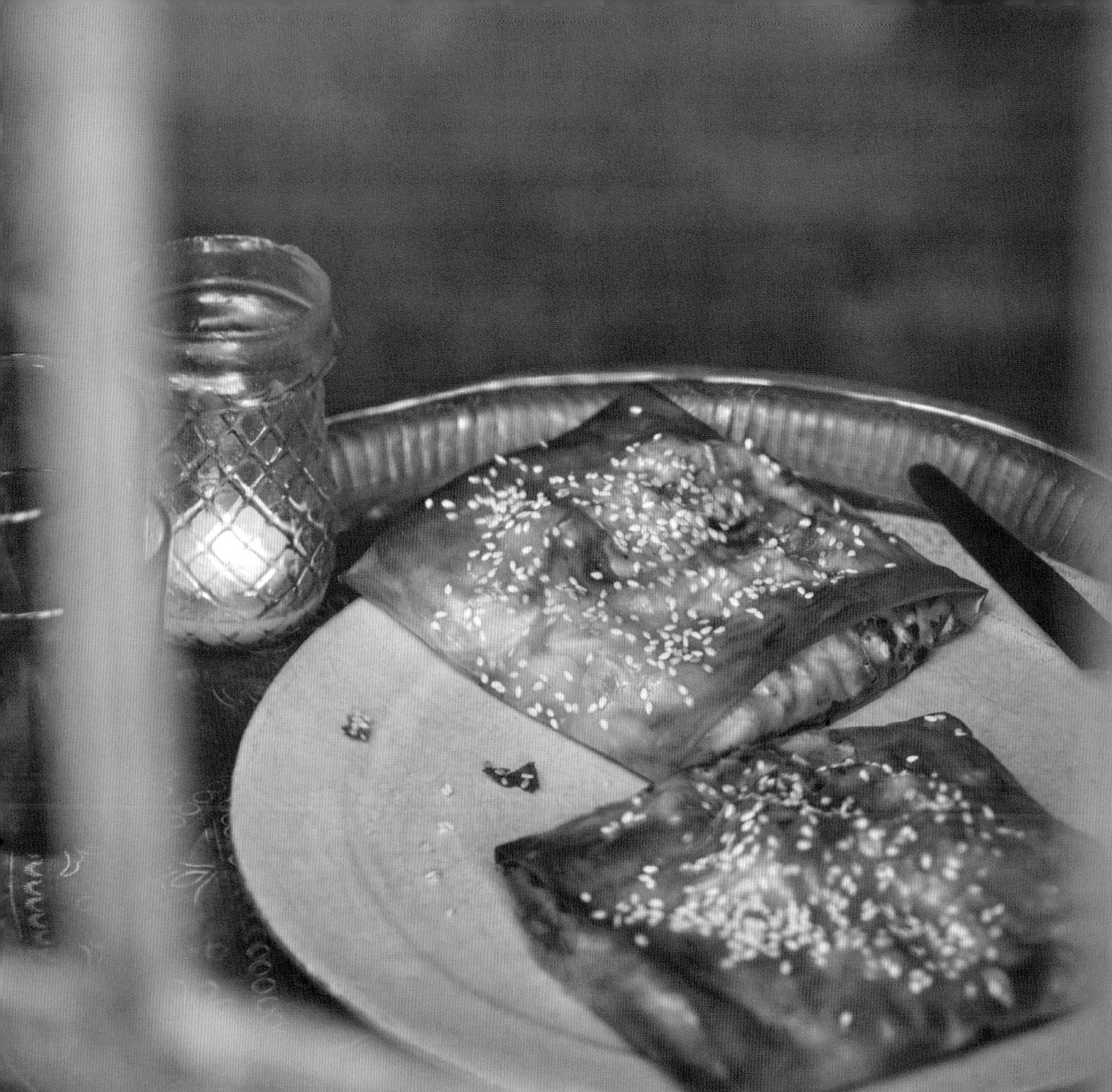

Working with one sheet at a time, brush lightly with oil. Take a portion of filling and place it on the phyllo about 3 inches from a short edge, forming it into a square shape, about 4 inches square. Bring the short edge up over the filling to partially cover, then fold the long sides over. Carefully turn the parcel to completely enclose the filling, resulting in a square-shaped packet. Brush lightly with oil between any bits of phyllo. Repeat to make six pies.

Brush the pies with the egg yolk glaze and sprinkle each with 1 tsp sesame seeds or nigella seeds. Bake for 25 minutes, until the pastry is crisp and golden. Serve hot.

SPICY FRIED GROUND BEEF ON A BED OF EGGPLANT AND YOGURT PURÉE

Turkish and Arab restaurants are primarily kebab houses that serve mezzes. The home-cooking equivalent of kofta kebab is fried ground meat. This interpretation of a Gaziantep specialty, with spices and pomegranate molasses, on a bed of creamy eggplant and yogurt purée, qualifies as Middle Eastern haute cuisine.

My granddaughter Sarah cooked this for her Cambridge engineering tutor, Jossy Sayir. He is also a foodie. He came to lunch in my garden with his daughters and his guitar and sang – beautifully. We had promised to invite him when we heard that one of his aunts in Istanbul had given me recipes that went into one of my old books.

Serves 4 to 6

4 eggplants (about 2¾ lb / 1.3kg)
2 cups / 480g Greek yogurt
salt and black pepper
1 to 2 garlic cloves, crushed (optional)
¼ cup / 60ml olive oil or sunflower oil
2 large onions, coarsely chopped
1 lb / 450g ground beef
1½ tsp ground cinnamon
¾ tsp ground allspice
1½ tbsp pomegranate molasses
1 good pinch Aleppo pepper (optional)
¼ cup / 60ml water
7 tbsp / 50g pine nuts, lightly toasted
1 large bunch flat-leaf parsley, leaves chopped
1 handful pomegranate seeds (optional)

Preheat the broiler to high. Prick each eggplant in several places with the point of a knife so that they don't burst when they cook. Place them on a baking sheet lined with foil. Cook under the broiler for about 30 minutes, turning them at least once, until the skins are blistered and black in parts and they feel very soft when you press them. Peel over a colander and chop and mash the flesh with a fork, letting the juices drain.

Put the yogurt in a bowl. Season with salt and black pepper, add the garlic (if using), and mix in the mashed eggplant.

In a wide skillet or sauté pan over low heat, warm the oil. Fry the onions, with the lid on, stirring often, for 20 minutes, until very soft and golden.

Add the meat to the pan and cook, crushing, chopping, and turning it over with a spatula until it changes color. Stir in the cinnamon, allspice, pomegranate molasses, Aleppo pepper (if using), and water and season with salt and black pepper. Cook for

15 to 20 minutes, stirring and turning the meat, until it is very soft. Stir in the pine nuts and parsley.

Spread the eggplant and yogurt purée in a serving dish and put the hot meat on top. If you like, sprinkle with the pomegranate seeds before serving.

MEATBALLS WITH SOUR CHERRIES

This is an old family dish that originates in Aleppo, Syria. In Egypt, my Aunt Regine served it at her buffet parties on a bed of toasted pita bread, cut into triangles. Her cook rolled the meat into tiny marble-size balls. It was exquisite. Regine went on to live in Paris, where I saw her often; many of the recipes in my first book came from her. I use dried pitted sour cherries, if I can find them, and serve it on plain rice.

Serves 4

½ cup / 90g dried pitted sour cherries
1¼ cups / 300ml water
juice of ½ lemon, or more to taste
14 oz / 400g lean ground lamb
1½ tsp ground cinnamon
½ tsp ground allspice
salt and black pepper
3 tbsp olive oil or sunflower oil
1 large onion, halved and sliced
1 good pinch Aleppo pepper (optional)

Put the dried cherries in a small pan with the water and lemon juice and simmer over low heat for 30 minutes, until the cherries are very soft and the liquid has reduced (adding a little water if it becomes too dry).

Put the lamb in a bowl, add the cinnamon and allspice, season with salt and black pepper, and use your hand to work to a soft paste. Take small pieces of the mixture, the size of a small walnut, and roll them into little balls between the palms of your hands.

In a large skillet or sauté pan over low heat, warm the oil. Add the onion and cook, stirring often, for about 5 minutes, until it softens.

Push the onion to one side of the pan and add the meatballs. Cook over medium-low heat for 8 to 10 minutes, turning the meatballs to brown them all over, and stirring and turning the onion until it is golden.

Pour the cherries with their liquid into the pan, season with salt and black pepper and the Aleppo pepper, if you like, and simmer for 5 minutes. Serve hot.

PORK MEATBALLS WITH CURRANTS AND PINE NUTS IN A CIDER SAUCE WITH CHESTNUTS

My favorite pork dishes are roast belly of pork – I love the melting tenderness – and meatballs, because they absorb sauces well. For these, I was inspired by the French sauté de porc au cidre with chestnuts and by Sicilian meatballs that have raisins and pine nuts worked into the meat.

Serves 4

¼ cup / 60ml sunflower oil or olive oil

2 onions, halved and sliced

1 lb / 450g ground pork

1 good pinch ground nutmeg

salt and black pepper

¼ cup / 35g currants or raisins, soaked in water for 30 minutes and then drained

¼ cup / 30g pine nuts

all-purpose flour for coating

1⅔ cups / 395ml medium-dry cider

one 6.5-oz / 184g package cooked whole chestnuts

In a large sauté pan over low heat, warm the oil. Fry the onions, stirring often, for about 10 minutes, until browned and beginning to caramelize, then remove them from the pan.

Put the pork in a bowl. Add the nutmeg, season with salt and pepper, and knead vigorously to achieve a soft, paste-like texture. Work in the drained currants or raisins and the pine nuts. Take small pieces of the meat mixture and roll into little balls the size of a large walnut, pressing them firmly between the palms of your hands.

Roll the meatballs in flour, put them in the sauté pan, and cook over medium heat, turning to lightly brown them all over. Add the cider and the chestnuts and return the fried onions to the pan. Simmer for 10 to 15 minutes, covered, adding salt and plenty of pepper and turning the meatballs over once, until they are cooked through. Serve the meatballs hot.

TINY TENDER LAMB CHOPS

A tour of kebab houses in Istanbul became a gastronomic marathon. At every stop, I was invited (practically forced) to eat. At the fifth restaurant, they opened a big refrigerated room and showed me all the prize cuts, which were later presented to me on a gigantic tray straight from the fire. As well as the usual kebabs on skewers, there were baby lamb chops, kidneys, slices of calf's liver, beef steaks, sucuk (spicy beef sausages), and pieces of chicken. It was a gourmand's dream, but for someone sitting alone at a table, already satiated from eating elsewhere and afraid to give offense, it was a nightmare.

In restaurants, I always go for the ground meat kofta kebab, but my favorite to make at home are the tiny, ever-so-tender rib chops cut from a rack of lamb. I make them for my granddaughter Lily. They are her favorite, too.

I serve them with herby mashed potatoes with olive oil (use half the quantity on page 123) or cucumber and tomato salad (page 84). You can garnish with watercress or radishes.

Serves 2 or 3

1 rack of lamb (6 to 7 chops), trimmed

1 tbsp olive oil

salt and black pepper

Cut the rack of lamb into chops, using a cleaver or heavy knife. Brush them all over with the olive oil.

Lightly oil a grill pan or heavy skillet and set over high heat. Cook the chops for 2 to 3 minutes on each side, until they are browned on the outside but still pink and juicy inside. Do not overcook them, they are best eaten slightly underdone. The meat is so good that all the cutlets need is a sprinkle of salt and pepper before serving.

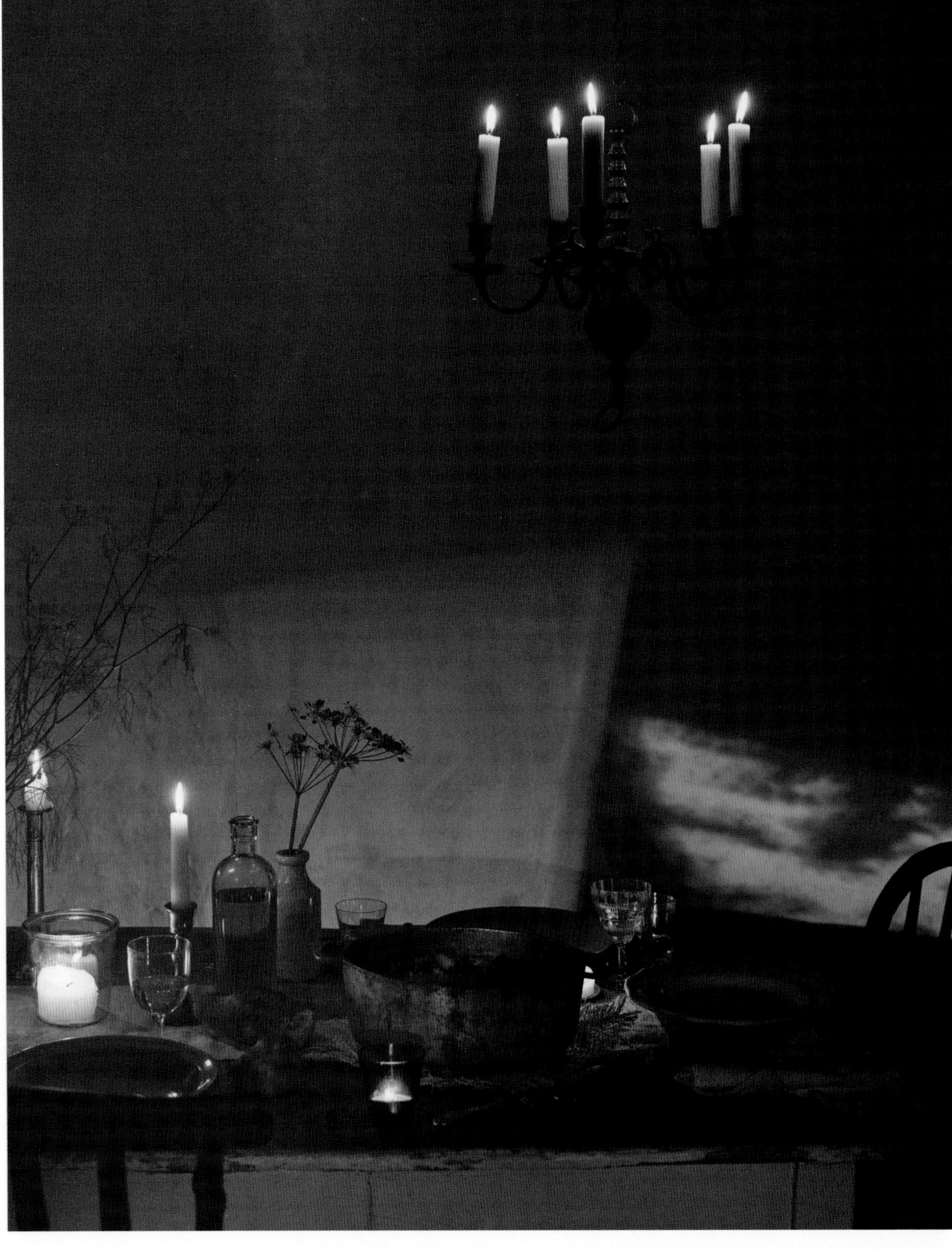

PROVENÇAL DAUBE

This famous Provençal stew, with the mingled flavors and aromas of red wine, meat juices, garlic, orange peel, herbs, and spices, is a marvelous winter dinner-party dish. It is very easy to make and can be left simmering gently for several hours – you do not need to watch it – and you can make it the day before.

In the nineteenth century, every inn in Provence had a pot of daube in the ashes of the fireplace, ready for hungry travelers stopping on their way. It was served with potatoes; and in places with Italian settlers, with polenta or macaroni.

Lamb – shoulder trimmed of fat or neck fillet cut into large pieces – is the traditional meat for the daube, but you can use beef – top round, bottom round, shank, or cheek trimmed of fat. Serve with potatoes, polenta (see page 228), or macaroni.

Serves 6 to 8

¼ cup / 60ml sunflower oil or olive oil

2 to 3½ lb / 1 to 1.5kg lamb or beef (see headnote), cut into large pieces

2 large onions, each cut into 6 wedges

4 oz / 130g unsmoked pancetta or diced bacon

5 garlic cloves, peeled

1 lb / 450g carrots, cut into slices ½ to ¾ inch thick

salt and black pepper

one 750ml bottle red wine

2 bay leaves

4 or 5 thyme sprigs

1 tsp ground cinnamon

¾ tsp ground allspice

3 or 4 whole cloves

2 to 3 tsp sugar

strips of peel from 1 orange

3 to 4 tbsp cognac or grappa (optional)

Warm the oil in a large heavy-bottomed pan or Dutch oven over medium heat. Add the lamb or beef and cook, turning the pieces to brown them all over.

Remove the meat to a plate and add the onions and pancetta or bacon to the pan. Sauté for about 6 minutes, stirring, until the onions are lightly colored and the pancetta or bacon releases its fat. Add the garlic for the last minute or so, then the carrots, and season with salt and black pepper.

Return the meat to the pan, pour in the wine, and add the bay leaves, thyme, cinnamon, allspice, cloves, sugar, and orange peel. Add water to cover, bring to a boil, then turn the heat to low, cover the pan, and simmer very gently (the daube should be barely trembling) for 2 to 3 hours, keeping the meat submerged, until it is so tender you can cut it with a spoon. Remove the orange peel and, if you like, stir in the cognac or grappa before serving.

BEAN STEW WITH CHORIZO AND BACON

My grandson Peter cooked this for us to test the recipe. The smell filled the house, and the taste . . . mmm. Spanish peasants used to dry their own beans and make their own chorizo with chopped pork meat and fat, garlic, and pimentón, which gives it a reddish color and strong distinctive flavor. There are many varieties of chorizo in different shapes and sizes, smoked or unsmoked, and with added herbs and seasonings. Fully cured chorizos are ready to eat; soft semi-cured ones need to be cooked. Any chorizo is great in this dish.

Serves 4

2 tbsp sunflower oil or olive oil

7 oz / 200g unsmoked slab bacon, cut into lardons, or pancetta

1 large onion, coarsely chopped

4 garlic cloves, chopped

¾ tsp ground cinnamon

¼ tsp ground allspice

1 tomato, peeled and chopped

two 15-oz / 425g cans butter beans or cannellini beans, drained and rinsed

9 oz / 250g chorizo, soft semi-cured or fully cured, mild or hot, cut into slices

2 cups / 480ml chicken stock

salt

4 thyme sprigs

extra-virgin olive oil for drizzling

Warm the oil in a wide pan over medium heat. Add the bacon or pancetta and onion and cook for about 10 minutes, stirring and turning over occasionally with a spatula, until the bacon or pancetta has released its fat and the onion is soft. Add the garlic and cook, stirring, until the onion is golden and the bacon is crisp.

Stir in the cinnamon, allspice, tomato, beans, and chorizo. Pour in the stock, add the thyme sprigs, and simmer over low heat for 15 minutes.

Season with salt, if necessary, bearing in mind that there is quite a bit of salt from the stock, chorizo, and bacon or pancetta. Serve hot, and pass around the extra-virgin olive oil for people to drizzle.

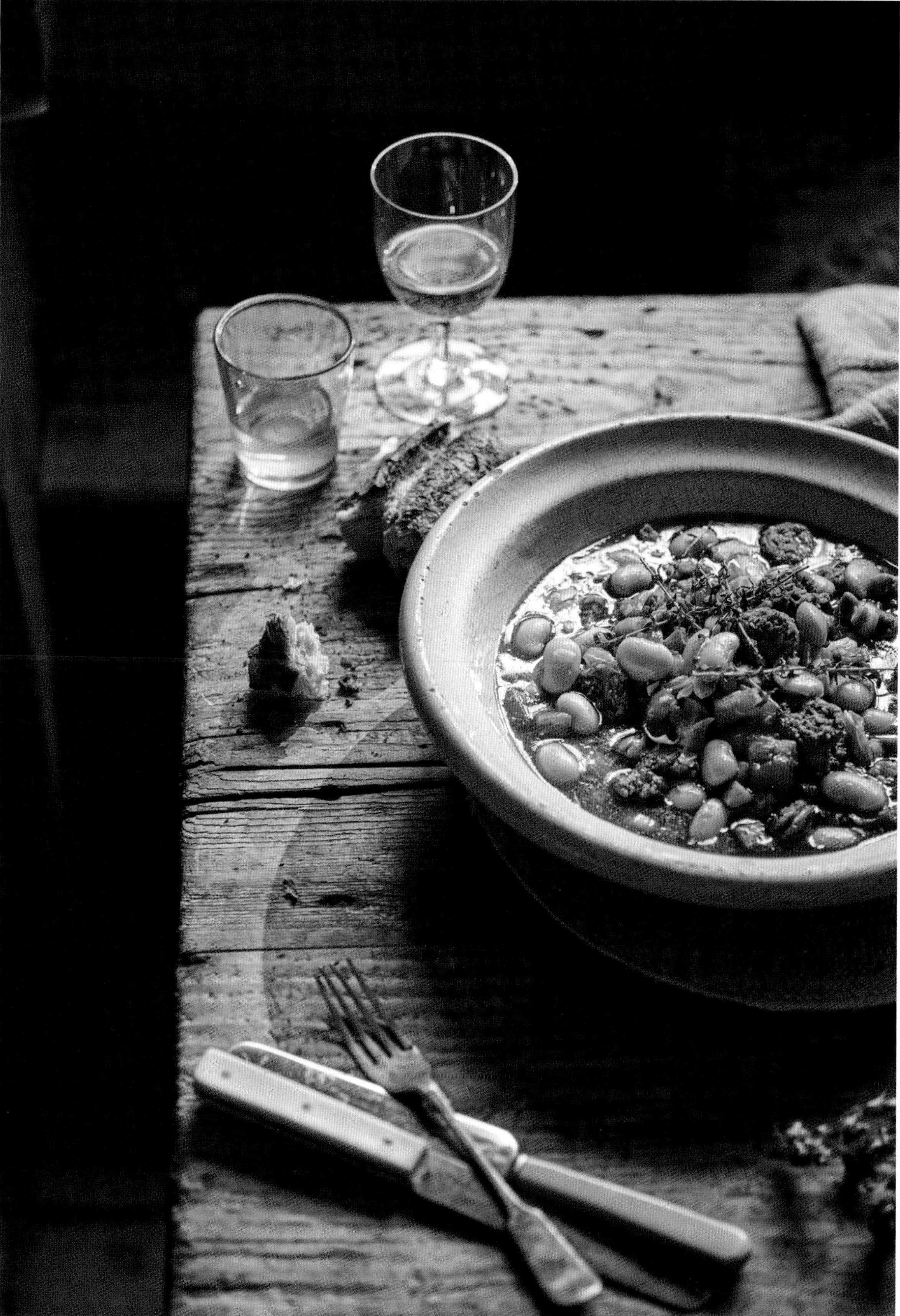

LAMB WITH HONEY AND ROSEMARY

This is a very delicately flavored stew; you would hardly know there was any honey. In Spain, they say that cordero al miel came with the Moors. In North Africa, where the Moors (Iberian Muslims) settled after their expulsion from Spain, causing a culinary revolution, they say the combination of lamb with honey is Andalusian. Sweet with savory is part of a Hispano-Arab style of cooking that developed during the centuries-long Muslim occupation of Spain. The South of France adopted the carré d'agneau au miel et romarin. My version is inspired by all three places. There is wine and just a touch of honey. A pinch of chili powder is the Spanish way of mitigating sweetness.

Lamb meat from the shoulder becomes meltingly tender without being stringy. A whole shoulder is very difficult to bone, so try to buy a boneless shoulder. Two lamb neck fillets will also do and need only 1 hour of cooking instead of the 2 hours for shoulder. Serve with boiled or mashed potatoes.

Serves 12

¼ cup / 60ml olive oil or sunflower oil

1¾ lb / 800g shallots, peeled

1 boneless shoulder of lamb, cut into large pieces

salt

4 rosemary sprigs, leaves finely chopped

1⅔ cups / 395ml dry white wine

3 tbsp brandy

1 tsp sugar

2 tbsp aromatic honey, such as orange blossom or acacia

black pepper or Aleppo pepper

Warm the oil in a large heavy-bottomed pan or Dutch oven over medium heat. Add the shallots and sauté for a few minutes, turning to brown them all over, then take them out and set aside.

Cook the lamb in batches in the same pan, turning the pieces to brown them all over. Return all the lamb to the pan, season with salt, and sprinkle the rosemary between layers of meat. Add the wine, brandy, and sugar and cover with about 1¼ cups / 300ml water.

Bring to a boil, then cover and simmer over low heat for 30 minutes. Put the browned shallots on top of the meat, add water to cover them, and continue to cook, covered, over low heat for 1 to 1½ hours, until the meat is so tender you can cut it with a spoon. About 10 minutes before the end, stir in the honey and some black pepper or Aleppo pepper. Taste and add more salt if necessary. Serve hot.

SLOW-ROASTED SHOULDER OF LAMB WITH COUSCOUS, DATES, AND ALMONDS

Shoulder of lamb is what I cook when I have many meat eaters to feed. Slow roasting makes the meat meltingly tender and juicy. I once made this shoulder with a date syrup glaze and couscous with dates for a dinner for artist Michael Rakowitz. His sculpture on the fourth plinth in Trafalgar Square – representing the ancient statue of the Lamassu, the winged bull with a human head that was destroyed by ISIS in Iraq – was made out of empty date-syrup tins. Dates have something of a sacred character in an Arab culture born in the desert. They symbolize hospitality and are said to have been a favorite food of the Prophet Muhammad. Their sweetness complements the sweetness of the meat. I love the combination.

I also serve slow-roasted shoulder of lamb with roasted vegetables (see pages 122 and 129), and the spiced saffron rice on page 153.

Serves 6 to 8

1 whole bone-in shoulder of lamb

salt and black pepper

1½ cups / 250g couscous

1½ cups / 360ml warm water

1 tbsp orange blossom water

1 tsp ground cinnamon

2 tbsp sunflower oil or vegetable oil

5½ oz / 155g pitted dates, cut into small pieces

6 tbsp / 50g raisins

3½ oz / 100g blanched almonds, coarsely chopped, plus 8 to 12 blanched whole almonds

2 tbsp date syrup, plus more for serving

4 tbsp / 60g butter, cut into small pieces

8 to 12 dates

Preheat the oven to 475°F.

Put the lamb shoulder, skin-side up, in a baking dish or roasting pan, sprinkle with salt and pepper, and roast in the hot oven for 20 minutes. Then turn the oven temperature to 325°F and cook for 4 hours, until the skin is crisp and browned and the meat is juicy and meltingly tender. Pour off the fat after about 2 hours.

Put the couscous in another baking dish, in which you can serve it. Combine the warm water, orange blossom water, and cinnamon and pour it over the couscous, stirring well so that the water is absorbed evenly. Let sit for about 10 minutes, then add the oil and rub the couscous between your hands above the dish to aerate the grains and break up any lumps.

Mix the dates, raisins, and chopped almonds into the couscous, cover with foil, and put in the oven with the lamb for the last 20 minutes, until it is steaming hot.

Before serving, pour the date syrup over the meat. Stir the butter into the couscous so that it melts in and is absorbed evenly. With a fork, fluff up the couscous, breaking up any lumps. Add a little salt, if necessary.

Remove the pits from each date and replace them with the whole blanched almonds; decorate the couscous with these dates. Serve the meat with the couscous. Pass date syrup around for people who may want some more.

de BUYER

GELATERIA

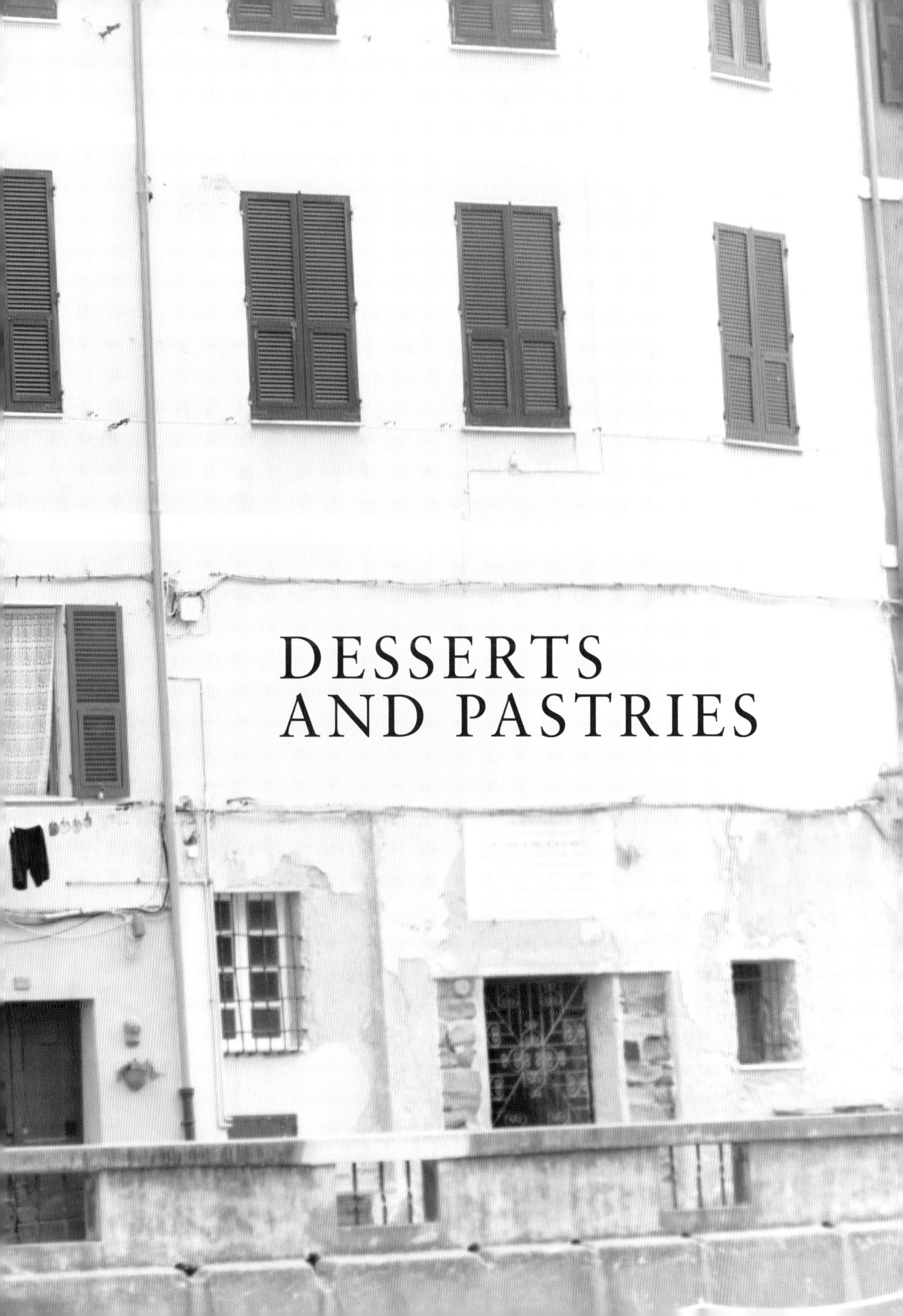

DESSERTS AND PASTRIES

The traditional Mediterranean way of ending a meal is with fresh fruit. I like simply cutting up different types of fruit and arranging them in slices on a large platter or making a fruit salad. I often serve orange slices with Medjool dates and pistachios, sometimes with a drop of orange blossom water or a dusting of cinnamon. I stuff pitted Medjool dates with walnut halves or with an almond or pistachio paste scented with rose water to serve with coffee or mint tea.

When I was a girl, the pastry I always longed for was a thick slice of bread soaked in caramel sugar syrup, topped with buffalo's milk cream so thick you could cut it with a knife. It is called aish el saraya (palace bread). I come from the sweet-toothed Arab Mediterranean world of phyllo and kadaifi pastries soaked in syrup, of candied fruits and fruit preserves and marzipan sweetmeats. I still make them – they are part of my happy childhood memories of visiting and entertaining and part of who I am.

But to end a meal, it is to France, Italy, and Spain that I usually turn. Most of the desserts in this chapter are with fruit, and many – the tarts, compotes, jellies, parfaits, chaussons, and the chestnuts in syrup – are French, inspired by what I eyed and often bought at patisseries and traiteurs in Paris. We can find all the Mediterranean fruits in Britain. Cooking them intensifies their flavors.

Arabs introduced milk puddings and almond pastries throughout the Mediterranean. You will find them in the following pages. But the flourless cakes with nuts and almonds are Passover cakes of the Sephardi Jews, whose ancestors, like mine, were banished from Spain and settled around the Mediterranean. They used ground nuts and almonds when their dietary laws forbade them flour or leaven.

FRESH BERRIES IN ORANGE CARAMEL SYRUP

Last summer, I managed to have regular deliveries of fresh berries straight from the farm. As a special dessert, I served them with an orange caramel syrup, which had an intense bitter-marmalade flavor, and orange-scented whipped cream.

Serves 4 to 6

1 cup / 240ml fresh orange juice

5 tbsp / 60g sugar

1 lb / 450g mixed berries, such as raspberries, blueberries, blackberries, strawberries

Bring the orange juice to a boil.

Cook the sugar in a pan over low heat and watch it as it becomes liquid and gradually turns caramel brown. Don't let it get too dark or it will be bitter. Take the pan off the heat for a moment or two and then gradually pour in the hot orange juice, stirring vigorously to dissolve the caramel, which will have hardened. Put back over low heat for 3 to 4 minutes, stirring, until the caramel is completely dissolved. Pour the syrup into a pitcher, let cool, then chill, covered, in the fridge.

Before serving, rinse the berries briefly. Hull any strawberries (if using) and cut them in half. Serve the berries in a bowl, pour the orange caramel syrup over them, and mix well.

Orange-flavored whipped cream

Whisk 1¼ cups / 300ml heavy cream until firm, then whisk in 2 tbsp sugar and the grated zest of 1 orange.

SWEET MUSCAT WINE GELATIN WITH MUSCAT GRAPES

This grown-up gelatin with jewel-like yellow and pink grapes is light and fresh with a deep flavor and intense aromatic scent. It is expensive but worth it for a special occasion.

Serves 4 to 6

one ¼-oz / 7g envelope unflavored gelatin

¼ cup / 60ml cold water

1½ cups / 355ml sweet Muscat or other dessert wine

10 oz / 285g Muscat grapes, washed

In a bowl, sprinkle the gelatin over the cold water. Gently whisk to combine and let sit for 5 minutes to soften.

Warm the wine over gentle heat but do not bring it to a boil. Pour the hot wine over the gelatin, stirring vigorously until the gelatin has dissolved.

Rinse a 4-cup / 950ml mold with cold water. Pour in the liquid gelatin and drop in the grapes. Let the gelatin cool, then cover and put in the fridge to set for at least 4 hours, or overnight.

When ready to serve, briefly lower the mold into a bowl of very hot water and then turn out onto a serving plate.

SANGRIA GELATIN

This festive gelatin is inspired by drinks I was served in a bar in Seville and it looks beautiful served in glass cups. It is great with port wine, but you can also make it with red or white wine, brandy, or rum.

Serves 6

2¼ tsp unflavored gelatin
5 tbsp / 75ml cold water
1¼ cups / 300ml port
1¼ cups / 300ml fresh orange juice
¼ cup / 50g sugar
2 apples, peeled and cut into small pieces
2 peaches, peeled and cut into small pieces

In a small bowl, sprinkle the gelatin over the water and let sit for about 5 minutes, until soft.

Warm the port, orange juice, and sugar over gentle heat, stirring to dissolve the sugar, but do not bring it to a boil. Pour the hot wine over the gelatin mixture, stirring vigorously until the gelatin has dissolved.

Put the apple and peach pieces in six cups or bowls and pour the liquid gelatin over them. Let the gelatin cool, then cover and put in the fridge to set for at least 4 hours, or overnight, before serving.

CHESTNUTS IN SYRUP

This sophisticated dessert is my idea of heaven. It is incredibly quick to make with precooked whole roasted chestnuts and is best done the day before or several hours in advance so that the chestnuts have time to absorb the alcohol. I use a very good cognac. I don't always use the whole amount of whipped cream to mix with the syrup, but keep some to float on coffee.

Serves 4

½ cup / 100g sugar

1 cup / 240ml water

½ tsp vanilla extract

one 6.5-oz / 184g package cooked whole chestnuts

3 tbsp cognac or rum

1¼ cups / 300ml heavy cream

Put the sugar, water, and vanilla in a pan over medium heat and simmer until the sugar has dissolved.

Add the chestnuts to the pan and cook for about 15 minutes, until they are soft and the syrup is reduced. Lift out the chestnuts with a slotted spoon and put them in a small bowl. Pour in the cognac or rum and refrigerate, covered. Keep the syrup in a separate container.

Using a whisk, whip the cream until it forms soft peaks, add the reserved syrup, and whip until stiff. Serve the chestnuts with the cream.

AMANDINES

I got this recipe thirty-five years ago from a baker in a village called Lumières in Provence – he was featured in BBC TV series *Claudia Roden's Mediterranean Cookery*. The original recipe had 2½ cups / 500g of sugar but many people now prefer less sugar – you can decrease the amount to 2 cups / 400g, depending on how sweet your tooth is. I still love it with 2½ cups / 500g. It is the favorite offering I bring to get-togethers when there are a lot of people. It is very rich, so I cut it into small pieces, but people always want more.

Makes about 49 small pieces

1 tbsp sunflower oil or vegetable oil

6 eggs

2¼ cups / 450g sugar

4 cups / 480g almond meal

¾ cup / 175ml whole milk

½ tsp vanilla extract

5 drops almond extract

¾ cup / 100g pine nuts

⅔ cup / 160ml apricot jelly or jam (optional)

Preheat the oven to 350°F. Line a shallow 12-inch square baking pan with parchment paper and brush with the oil.

Using a fork, lightly beat the eggs with the sugar and then add the almond meal, milk, vanilla, and almond extract and mix thoroughly. Pour into the prepared pan. Sprinkle the pine nuts on top and bake for 1 hour, until the top is brown and the cake feels firm. If it is brown too early, cover with foil.

If you wish, while the cake is still warm, melt the jelly or jam with 1 to 2 tbsp water and brush it over the top. Let cool.

Cut into squares with a sharp knife and lift out the amandines one by one to serve.

QUINCE PURÉE

You can usually find quinces in Middle Eastern and Asian shops in the winter months. I keep them in the kitchen for days for their heavenly scent, and when I cook them the fragrance fills the house. Eating them like this, simply mashed with a little sugar, is pure joy. I serve the purée with the whipped cream below, or with cheese – it is good with Pecorino sardo, Parmesan or Grana Padano, and with blue cheese or goat cheese.

Serves 6 to 8

3 quinces (about 2½ lb / 1.1kg total weight)

½ cup / 100g sugar

Preheat the oven to 300°F.

Wash the quinces, scrubbing them if they have down on their skins. Put them on a foil-lined baking sheet and bake for about 2 hours (the time depends on the size and ripeness of the fruit), until they are soft enough that you can easily pierce through to the center with a knife. Let cool.

Peel the quinces, cut them in half, and cut out the cores. It is messy but worth it. Put the flesh in a pan and cut it into pieces. Add the sugar and mash with a potato masher. Cook over low heat, stirring for about 5 minutes. Pour the purée into a serving dish and let cool, then cover and chill in the fridge before serving.

Rose-flavored whipped cream

Whisk 1¼ cups / 300ml heavy cream until almost firm, then stir in 2 tbsp sugar and 2 to 3 tsp rose water and whisk until firm.

Alternatively, instead of rose water, add ¼ tsp vanilla extract.

APPLE CHAUSSONS

There are several patisseries near my studio on Rue Saint-Dominique in Paris. One of them sells homey regional specialties and I can't resist heading there to get a chausson aux pommes. It is my guilty secret. My version is richer; I hope you will try it.

Makes 8 pastries

14-oz / 400g all-butter puff pastry sheet

4 medium apples

1 tbsp lemon juice

7 tbsp / 100ml apple cider or water

4 to 5 tbsp / 50 to 60g sugar, to taste

5 egg yolks

⅓ cup / 80ml crème fraîche or heavy cream

confectioners' sugar for dusting

Take the puff pastry out of the fridge and out of its package 20 minutes before you want to use it so that it is pliable and does not crack when you unroll it.

Peel, core, and quarter the apples, dropping them into a bowl of water with the lemon juice to stop them from discoloring. Drain them and put them in a pan with the cider or water, put the lid on, and cook over low heat for 10 to 15 minutes, until they are very soft. Remove the lid and simmer for a few minutes until all the liquid has evaporated.

Mash the apples with a potato masher, stir in the sugar, and cook over medium heat, stirring, for 2 to 3 minutes to allow more liquid to evaporate.

Beat four of the egg yolks with the crème fraîche or heavy cream. Add to the apple purée and cook over low heat, stirring vigorously, for 1 to 2 minutes, until the mixture thickens slightly. Let cool.

Preheat the oven to 400°F and lightly oil a large baking sheet. Mix the remaining egg yolk with a drop of water.

Unroll the pastry on the baking sheet and cut it into eight rectangles. Lightly brush the tops with the egg yolk glaze and bake for 20 minutes, until puffed up and browned.

Let the pastries cool slightly, then slice them through the middle with a serrated knife and fill each one with about 3 tbsp of the apple cream. Dust with confectioners' sugar before serving.

SWEET CHEESE MILLE-FEUILLES

These are like apple chaussons (see page 282) but with a cheese filling. They should be eaten hot or warm. You can make them in advance and reheat before serving. Eat them with your hands, like a sandwich.

Makes 8 pastries

12-oz / 340g all-butter puff pastry sheet
1 egg yolk, plus 1 egg
9 oz / 255g mozzarella (not di bufala)
5 tbsp / 60g sugar
grated zest of 1 orange
confectioners' sugar for dusting

Take the puff pastry out of the fridge and out of its package 20 minutes before you want to use it so that it is pliable and does not crack when you unroll it.

Preheat the oven to 400°F. Lightly oil a large baking sheet. Mix the egg yolk with a drop of water.

Unroll the pastry onto the baking sheet and cut it into eight rectangles. Lightly brush the tops with a little of the egg yolk glaze and bake for 10 minutes, until puffed up and lightly browned. Let cool slightly.

Cut the mozzarella into pieces and blend to a creamy paste with the sugar, orange zest, and egg.

When the pastries have cooled a little, slice them through the middle with a serrated knife and fill each one with about 2 tbsp of the filling. Turn them over, brush the new tops with the remaining egg yolk glaze, and bake for about 15 minutes, until browned.

Serve the pastries hot, turned over again, dusted with confectioners' sugar.

APPLE PARFAIT WITH CALVADOS

I buy Calvados, the apple brandy, mainly to put in apple desserts, such as crumbles, omelets, and pancakes. Its sweet aroma adds to the pleasure of this lovely French dessert. A *parfait* is still-frozen and does not need to be churned.

Serves 6

4 Golden Delicious apples, peeled, cored, and sliced

⅔ cup / 160ml dry white wine

½ cup / 100g sugar

3 egg yolks

3 tbsp Calvados or rum

⅔ cup / 160ml heavy cream

Put the apples and wine in a pan over low heat and simmer, covered, for 5 to 10 minutes, until the apples are soft.

Remove the lid and turn up the heat. Add ¼ cup / 50g of the sugar, mash the apples with a potato masher or fork, and cook, stirring, until the apple purée is thick and most of the liquid has evaporated.

Beat the egg yolks with the remaining ¼ cup / 50g sugar, until thick and pale. Pour into the apple purée, off the heat, stirring vigorously, then stir over low heat for 30 seconds. Stir in the Calvados or rum, let cool, and then chill in the fridge.

Whip the cream until firm and then fold into the cold apple purée. Line a bowl with plastic wrap (it makes turning out easier) and pour in the apple mixture. Cover the top with plastic wrap and freeze overnight.

Serve the parfait straight from the freezer. Remove the covering plastic wrap, turn out onto a serving plate, and remove the remaining plastic wrap.

Variation

~ Pears may be used instead of apples, with kirsch or Poire William brandy in place of the Calvados or rum.

PARFAIT MOCHA PRALINÉ

This very easy no-churn ice cream has the wonderful mix of coffee and praline flavors that I love and also brings back many happy memories. The same ingredients, plus ladyfingers, were those of a cake my mother always made for my father's birthday. When I went back to Egypt for the first time after thirty years, I looked in the window of the old pastry shop near where I used to live and there was the French cake book open to the page with our diplomate mocha praliné. My mother had ordered it there and learned to make it herself after she left Egypt.

Serves 8 to 10

scant ½ cup / 50g blanched hazelnuts

¼ cup / 50g sugar

1¼ cups / 300ml heavy cream

generous ½ cup / 175g sweetened condensed milk

2 tbsp instant espresso powder

Line a baking sheet with parchment paper.

In a dry skillet (not a nonstick one) over medium heat, toast the hazelnuts, shaking the pan, until they just begin to color. Tip the hazelnuts onto a plate and set aside.

Put the sugar in the pan, spread it out, and place over medium heat until it becomes liquid and turns a light golden color (watch it as it can quickly turn very dark and bitter). Put the hazelnuts back in and stir them around until they are well coated with the liquid caramel. When the caramel turns brown, pour it onto the lined baking sheet. Let it cool completely. When this praliné is hard and brittle, grind in a food processor.

Whisk the cream with the condensed milk and espresso powder until soft peaks form. Fold in the praliné, keeping 2 tbsp aside in a little cup covered with plastic wrap until you are ready to serve.

Line a loaf pan with plastic wrap (it makes turning out easier) and pour in the cream mixture. Cover the top with plastic wrap and freeze for at least 6 hours, or overnight.

Take the parfait out of the freezer 15 minutes before serving. Dip the loaf pan into a bowl of very hot water for a few seconds. Remove the covering plastic wrap. Turn the loaf pan upside down onto a serving plate and remove the remaining plastic wrap.

Serve the parfait sprinkled with the reserved praliné.

ROAST PEACHES WITH SWEET WINE, CLOTTED CREAM, AND CARAMELIZED PISTACHIOS

When the fruits we buy have not ripened on a tree, roasting is a way of bringing out the most they can offer. The sensual pleasure of this combination of roasted peaches with clotted cream and caramelized pistachios is immense. Use ripe but not soft peaches.

Serves 4

4 peaches, unpeeled, cut in half and pits removed

½ cup / 120ml sweet white wine

5 tbsp / 60g sugar

scant ½ cup / 60g pistachios

½ cup / 120g clotted cream

Preheat the oven to 375°F.

Arrange the peaches in a shallow baking dish, cut-sides up. Pour the sweet wine over them, so that a little settles in the hollows. Roast for about 30 minutes (the time depends on the size and ripeness of the fruit), until very tender when you pierce one with a knife. Let them cool, then chill, covered, in the fridge.

Line a baking sheet with parchment paper. Cook the sugar in a small pan over medium heat and watch it as it becomes liquid and gradually turns brown, the color of dark honey. Don't let it get too dark.

Quickly add the pistachios to the pan and stir until they are entirely coated with caramel, then pour onto the lined baking sheet. Let cool completely. When the caramel is cold, hard, and brittle, lift it off the baking sheet and coarsely chop.

Spread some clotted cream over each half peach and sprinkle with the caramelized pistachios before serving.

Variations

~ Instead of sweet wine, use dry white wine and 1 to 2 tbsp sugar.

~ Instead of clotted cream, use whipped cream or plain Greek yogurt.

NADIA'S GRANITAS

My daughter Nadia, an artist, designer, and film animator, was named "Ice Princess" in New York when she wrote a book, *Granita Magic*, and sold her homemade ice pops on the High Line, a park built on a disused overhead railway line in Manhattan. Now that she lives in London, she makes granitas for the family and creates ice-pop recipes for my grandson Cesar's Ice Kitchen. The pear and anise granita is also nice served with cream.

Each granita serves 6 to 8

Orange and lemon

1¼ cups / 300ml water

scant ¾ cup / 140g sugar

3¾ cups / 890ml fresh orange juice

3 tbsp fresh lemon juice

1 tbsp orange blossom water

Pear and anise

1¼ cups / 300ml water

3 star anise

½ cup / 100g sugar

juice of 1 lemon

5 flavorful pears, peeled, cut into eighths, and cored

Milk and honey

3½ cups / 830ml whole milk

6 to 7 tbsp honey

4 cardamom pods, crushed

2 tbsp rose water

To make the orange and lemon granita mixture, put the water and sugar in a small pan and simmer just until the sugar dissolves. Take off the heat and stir in the orange juice, lemon juice, and orange blossom water.

To make the pear and anise granita mixture, put the water, star anise, sugar, and lemon juice in a pan and add the pears. Bring to a boil, then simmer gently, covered, for 5 to 8 minutes, until the pears are tender. Take off the heat and let cool for 20 minutes. Remove the star anise and blend the mixture to a smooth purée.

To make the milk and honey granita mixture, put ¾ cup / 175ml of the milk, the honey, and cardamom pods in a small pan and simmer gently, stirring, just until the honey dissolves. Take off the heat and let infuse for 20 minutes. Strain the mixture into a bowl; discard the cardamom. Stir in the remaining milk and the rose water.

Pour the granita mixture into a wide, shallow container, cover, and freeze for 3 to 4 hours, then scrape and crush the ice with a fork. Repeat this process every hour or so, at least three times, until the mixture has turned into small sequin-like ice flakes.

Before serving, rake the granita up again with the fork to lighten the texture. It's best eaten within a day or two, but will stay fresh for longer in an airtight freezer container.

ANDALUSIAN RAISIN AND SWEET WINE ICE CREAM

I discovered this splendid ice cream when I was researching the cuisines of Spain. Raisins soaked in sweet dark wine are mixed into the rich vanilla ice cream when it is almost firm, and the same wine is passed around for pouring over.

Serves 10

¾ cup / 105g raisins or currants

one 750ml bottle sweet Pedro Ximénez sherry or Malaga Moscatel wine

3 cups / 720ml heavy cream

1¼ cups / 300ml whole milk

1 small cinnamon stick

few drops vanilla extract

8 egg yolks

½ cup / 100g sugar

Put the raisins or currants in a small bowl, pour in 7 tbsp / 100ml of the sherry or wine and let soak.

In a medium saucepan, combine the cream, milk, cinnamon stick, and vanilla and warm until almost boiling. Remove from the heat and let infuse for 30 minutes before removing the cinnamon stick. Reheat the milk.

Using an electric hand mixer, beat the egg yolks with the sugar until pale and thick. Add a ladleful of hot milk and whisk well, then pour the mixture into the milk pan, off the heat, and stir vigorously with a wooden spoon. Place the pan in a large saucepan of boiling water over medium heat, and stir constantly until the mixture thickens enough to coat the spoon. Do not let this custard boil or it will curdle. (If it does curdle, you can save it by beating thoroughly with the hand mixer until it is smooth.)

Pour the custard into a serving bowl and let it cool, then cover with plastic wrap and put into the freezer. After 3 to 3½ hours, when it is firm but not yet hard, take it out of the freezer and mix in the raisins with their liquid. You must do this before the ice cream becomes too hard to mix but is firm enough that the raisins remain suspended evenly and do not sink to the bottom. If you do not mix thoroughly, there will be little white lumps in the ice cream but that, too, is lovely. If you want to serve the ice cream turned out onto a plate, transfer the custard to a mold lined with plastic wrap and cover. Return it to the freezer for at least 6 hours, or overnight.

Take the ice cream out of the freezer. Remove the covering and dip the mold into a bowl of hot water for a few seconds. Turn the mold upside down on the serving plate and remove the remaining plastic wrap. Pass the bottle of sherry or wine for everyone to drizzle a little over their ice cream.

RICE PUDDING WITH FRUIT IN SYRUP

Rice pudding is much loved everywhere around the Mediterranean in a variety of flavors – vanilla, orange, cinnamon, cardamom, honey. I love them all, but I have a special affection for mastic. It gives this pudding a delicious and intriguing taste. Mastic is the resin from a tree that grows on the Greek island of Chios. You can buy it in small grains or crystals in Greek and Middle Eastern stores. You have to crush and grind them to a powder with ½ tsp sugar, using a mortar and pestle. Use very little, otherwise the taste is unpleasant. The variation with cardamom is great, too.

Serves 8 to 10

¾ cup / 150g risotto rice or short-grain rice

1½ cups / 360ml water

4 cups / 950ml whole milk

½ to ¾ cup / 100 to 150g sugar, to taste

2 tbsp rose water

½ tsp ground mastic (from about 4 mastic crystals)

Poached fruits in syrup

¾ cup / 150g caster sugar

2 cups / 480ml water

1 tsp fresh lemon juice

½ tsp vanilla extract

12 cardamom pods, cracked

4 pears, peeled, quartered, and cored

8 apricots or greengage plums, cut in half and pits removed

Combine the rice and water in a large pan. Bring to a boil and simmer for 8 minutes, until the water has been absorbed. Add the milk and simmer over very low heat, stirring occasionally, for 35 minutes, until the rice is very soft. Add ½ cup / 100g of the sugar and cook, stirring until dissolved. Taste and add more sugar, if necessary. There should still be some liquid in the pan (the pudding will firm as it cools and should be very creamy). Add the rose water and vigorously stir in the mastic, then take off the heat. Pour into a shallow serving dish and let cool.

For the poached fruits, combine the sugar, water, and lemon juice in a pan and bring to a simmer. Add the vanilla and cardamom. Drop in the pears and simmer for 8 minutes, until just tender. Add the apricots or plums and cook for 2 minutes more. Lift the fruit out of the syrup onto a plate, to remove the excess syrup.

Serve the rice pudding paired with the poached fruit.

Variation

~ Omit the mastic and add ten cracked cardamom pods to steep in the milk.

LEMON TART

Around the corner from my studio in Paris, I often stop to buy a tarte au citron at the patisserie in the Rue de Bourgogne. My version has an intensely lemony crème au citron filling. It is worth making the sweet biscuity pâte sucrée if you have time, but if you are in a hurry you can use a good store-bought piecrust.

Serves 6 to 8

Pâte sucrée

1⅔ cups / 200g all-purpose flour

½ cup / 50g confectioners' sugar

7 tbsp / 100g cold unsalted butter, cut into pieces

1 egg yolk

Lemon filling

6 tbsp / 85g unsalted butter

grated zest of 1 lemon, plus 5 tbsp / 75ml fresh lemon juice

9½ tbsp / 120g sugar

2 eggs

To make the pâte sucrée, combine the flour and confectioners' sugar in a bowl. Using your fingertips, rub the butter into the flour until crumbly. Stir in the egg yolk with a fork. If the dough is still dry, stir in 1 to 2 tbsp cold water until it holds together. Press into a ball, flatten it, and wrap in plastic wrap or wax paper, then chill for 30 minutes.

Preheat the oven to 400°F and lightly grease a 9-inch round tart pan with a removable bottom.

Line the pan with the pastry, pressing it firmly up the sides with the palm of your hand (with this soft dough, it's easier than rolling). Prick all over the bottom of the pastry with a fork. Bake for 15 to 17 minutes, until golden brown. Let cool.

For the lemon filling, melt the butter in a heavy-bottomed pan. Take the pan off the heat and add the lemon zest, lemon juice, sugar, and eggs. Whisking vigorously, bring to a simmer over low heat, and continue whisking until it is the thickness of honey, about 30 seconds. Cover and refrigerate until ready to use.

Pour the filling into the tart shell and chill for 1 hour before serving.

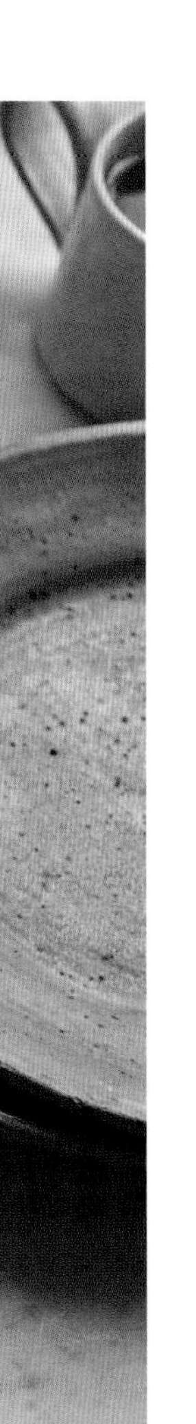

PLUM CLAFOUTIS

I have made many clafoutis over the years. For this book, I tried this famous French baked dessert again with different fruits and batters. When cherries, the traditional fruit, were in season, I didn't want to cook them. They were too good and too expensive. I just wanted to eat them. My favorite clafoutis was with red, purple, or greengage plums in a light custard perfumed with vanilla and rum. I hope you will love it, too.

Serves 6 to 8

1¾ lb / 800g red, purple, or greengage plums

½ cup / 120ml whole milk

½ cup / 120ml heavy cream

4 eggs

½ cup / 100g granulated sugar

1 tbsp all-purpose flour

½ tsp vanilla extract

3 tbsp rum

1 tbsp confectioners' sugar

Preheat the oven to 350°F. Butter a shallow 11-inch round baking dish.

Wash and dry the plums, cut them in half, and remove the pits. Arrange them cut-side down in the baking dish; they should fit snugly.

Bring the milk and cream to a boil in a pan, then remove from the heat.

Beat the eggs with the granulated sugar and flour until well blended, then stir in the vanilla and rum. Pour the hot milk into the mixture, whisking continuously, then pour over the fruit. Bake for 45 minutes, until set.

Serve the clafoutis dusted with the confectioners' sugar. It's best eaten warm, not hot.

ALMOND PUDDING WITH APRICOT COMPOTE

Milk puddings thickened with cornstarch are traditional dishes with an old history in almost every country around the Mediterranean. There are also versions with added ground almonds. This is the Sicilian biancomangiare di mandorle, with a floral perfume and subtle bitter-almond flavor, paired with a sharp apricot compote.

Serves 6 to 8

2 cups / 480ml whole milk

¼ cup / 35g cornstarch

½ cup / 100g sugar

6½ tbsp / 50g almond meal

3 tbsp pistachios, finely chopped

3 to 4 drops (no more) almond extract

1½ tbsp orange blossom water or rose water

Apricot compote

2¼ lb / 1kg apricots, cut in half and pits removed

⅔ cup / 160ml water

½ cup / 100g sugar

1 tsp vanilla extract

Pour 1½ cups / 360ml of the milk into a pan and bring to a simmer. Mix the cornstarch with the remaining ½ cup / 120ml milk, stirring vigorously until it is completely dissolved.

As the milk in the pan reaches the simmering point, lower the heat and vigorously whisk in the milk-cornstarch mixture. Continue to whisk constantly for 2 to 3 minutes, until it comes back to a simmer and becomes a thick cream.

Stir the sugar, almond meal, pistachios, and almond extract into the milk and continue to cook over low heat for 12 minutes. Stir in the orange blossom water or rose water and pour into individual glass bowls or cups. Chill, covered, in the fridge.

For the compote, put the apricots, cut-side up, in a wide pan with a tight-fitting lid, add the water, and sprinkle the sugar between the layers. Put the lid on and set the pan over high heat. The apricots will soften in about 5 minutes and produce a lot of juice. Add the vanilla and continue to cook with the lid off, stirring often, for another 5 minutes, until the apricots have collapsed. Let cool. If you are making it in advance, keep covered in the fridge.

When serving, spoon some apricot compote on top of the almond pudding.

YOGURT CAKE

This Turkish cake is like a light, airy, fresh-tasting cheesecake. We make it all the time in my family, and you really must try it.

Serves 6 to 8

4 eggs, separated

½ cup / 100g sugar

3 tbsp all-purpose flour

1⅔ cups / 400g whole-milk Greek yogurt

grated zest and juice of 1 unwaxed lemon

Preheat the oven to 350°F. Butter a 9-inch round nonstick cake pan with a removable bottom.

Using an electric hand mixer, beat the egg whites until soft peaks form.

In another bowl, using the same mixer, beat the egg yolks with the sugar until thick and pale. Add the flour, yogurt, lemon zest, and lemon juice and beat to a homogenous cream.

Gently fold the egg whites into the yogurt mixture and pour into the prepared pan. Bake for 40 to 45 minutes, until the top is lightly browned – watch it carefully for the last few minutes of cooking so that it doesn't brown too much. The cake will puff up like a soufflé and then subside. Let it cool a little before lifting it out onto a serving plate.

Serve the cake warm or cold.

Macerated strawberries

For a beautiful accompaniment to the yogurt cake, briefly rinse 1 lb / 450g strawberries, hull, and cut them in half through the stem end, then sprinkle with 5 tbsp / 60g superfine sugar and the juice of ½ lemon and let sit for 1 hour before serving.

HAZELNUT CAKE WITH CHOCOLATE GANACHE

Hazelnuts and chocolate are traditional partners and they work beautifully in this hazelnut cake topped with a thick layer of luscious chocolate ganache. If you don't have an 8-inch cake pan, you can use a larger one; I have also made this in a 9-inch pan.

Serves 12

6 egg whites

6 tbsp / 75g superfine sugar

9 oz / 255g blanched hazelnuts, coarsely ground

Ganache

1 cup / 240ml heavy cream

8 oz / 225g best-quality dark chocolate (70% cacao), broken into small pieces

Preheat the oven to 350°F. Butter and flour an 8-inch round nonstick cake pan with a removable bottom.

Using an electric hand mixer, beat the egg whites until stiff and then gradually and gently fold in the sugar and ground hazelnuts.

Pour the mixture into the prepared pan and bake for 45 to 60 minutes, until pale golden and firm to the touch. Let cool before lifting it out of the pan.

For the ganache, pour the cream into a pan and bring to a boil, then take off the heat. Add the chocolate and let stand for 5 minutes until it softens, then beat with a whisk or a spatula until thoroughly blended. Let cool slightly until thick but still pourable.

When ready to serve, spread the ganache over the top of the cake.

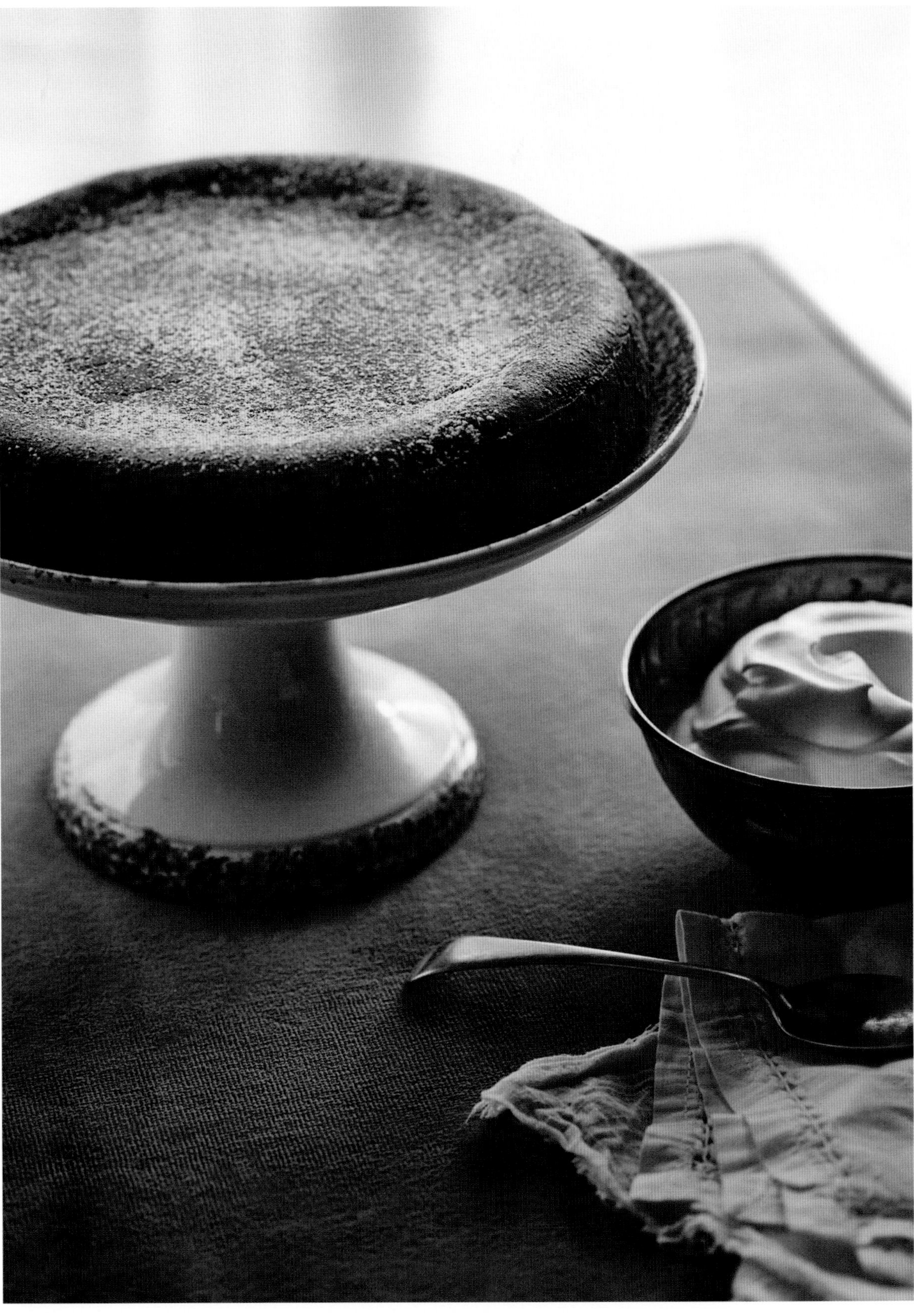

CHOCOLATE CAKE

Our all-time-favorite family birthday cake is a Sephardi Jewish Passover cake. I got the recipe from my mother's friend Lucie Ades, whose family came from France and was of Spanish ancestry. I am guessing that they were from Bayonne in Southwest France, where Jews fleeing the Inquisition in the early sixteenth century settled and started the first chocolate manufacturing industry. It is there that chocolate cakes with almonds first appeared. I have always made this with the Menier Chocolat Patissier that I find at my supermarket. Serve it with clotted cream or whipped cream.

Serves 12

7 oz / 200g best-quality dark chocolate (70% cacao), broken into pieces

6 eggs, separated

6 tbsp / 75g granulated sugar

generous ¾ cup / 100g almond meal

confectioners' sugar for dusting (optional)

Preheat the oven to 350°F. Butter and flour a 9-inch round nonstick cake pan with a removable bottom.

Melt the chocolate in a heatproof bowl placed over a pan of boiling water so that the bowl does not touch the water.

Using an electric hand mixer, beat the egg whites until stiff.

In another bowl, using the same mixer, beat the egg yolks with the granulated sugar until pale. Mix in the almond meal and then the melted chocolate. Add 1 to 2 tbsp of the beaten whites and mix them in to loosen the very dense almond-chocolate mixture, then fold in the remaining whites.

Pour the mixture into the prepared pan and bake for 30 minutes, until firm to the touch. Let cool before removing from the pan.

When ready to serve, dust the cake with confectioners' sugar, if you like.

WALNUT CAKE

This cake is as delicious as it is simple, with a pure walnut flavor complemented by an orange fragrance – a traditional Mediterranean combination. You must make sure the walnuts aren't stale, as they have a tendency to become rancid. These quantities yield a thin cake, about ¾ inch thick – you can double them if you want a larger cake, using a 10- or 11-inch round pan. It is a perfect quick teatime cake.

Serves 4 to 6

1¼ cups / 125g walnuts

2 eggs

10 tbsp / 125g granulated sugar

grated zest of 1 orange

confectioners' sugar for dusting

Preheat the oven to 400°F. Butter a 8- or 9-inch round nonstick cake pan or tart pan with a removable bottom.

Put the walnuts in a food processor and grind, not too finely; set aside.

Using an electric hand mixer, beat the eggs with the granulated sugar until pale and thick. Add the orange zest and then fold in the walnuts until well mixed.

Pour the mixture into the prepared pan and bake for 40 minutes, until firm to the touch. Let cool before removing from the pan.

When ready to serve, dust the cake with confectioners' sugar.

INDEX

R

ACKNOWLEDGMENTS

I thank the friends who came to dinner over the years and helped me choose the recipes that went into this book. My family have always been regulars at my table, and in the final months before handing in the manuscript, my children and grandchildren offered to test recipes. Everyone took to cooking passionately. Their names are in my dedication. Thank you all for your feedback and enthusiasm. You have helped make the book what it is.

My warmest thanks go to the friends far away who offered to test recipes. I appreciated their checking and comments hugely. Writer Adina Hoffman in New Haven, Connecticut, whom I got to know at Yale, also gave an American perspective. I often turned to her and her husband, poet Peter Cole, for general advice. Jonah Freud, who is translating *Mediterranean* into Dutch and is the owner of the best cookbook shop in Amsterdam, tested while on a canal journey in France. She is a fantastic cook and food writer, as well as a fount of culinary knowledge for chefs and food writers who come to her for advice. Gabrielle Sachs, who is married to my cousin Dov and lives in Bordeaux, is a cardiology nurse renowned for her cooking and the most passionate home cook I know. She brought a French lens to the recipes and was my "super tester." I could hardly keep up with her requests for more recipes to try, and waited for her comments and suggestions, hoping for a "Délicieux! Dov a adoré."

I am more grateful than I can say to my agent Lizzy Kremer for her warm friendship and unstinting support over many years, and for her encouragement, advice, and championing of this book. Thank you also for testing recipes, Lizzy; your comments were a great help. Working with you is a huge privilege and a joy. I thank Maddalena Cavaciuti, Lizzy's assistant at David Higham, for testing, too. I valued her Italian know-how.

I am thrilled and delighted with the beautiful book that Ebury has produced, and thank Andrew Goodfellow, Lizzy Gray, Laura Higginson, and Celia Palazzo for wanting to make it the best it could be. I feel lucky and grateful to be published by you. I have special thanks for Andrew for the title, and for Celia, my editor, for making it all happen and for bringing together the dream team that created it. I have many thanks, too, for Emily Brickell, who took over when Celia left to have her baby.

I am full of admiration and especially grateful to Emily Preece-Morrison, indefatigable editor and project manager, for her care and dedication, for the brilliant way she captured the spirit of the book, inspired the creative team, and got it all to work. I thank copy editor Maggie Ramsay for her eagle eye and attention to detail; Frankie Unsworth, the amazing food and props stylist, for creating the feel of the Mediterranean for the shoots; and to her assistant Izy Hossack for the cooking.

I love Susan Bell's lyrical photography. She has a magic touch. Her photos of food are both simple and seductive and make you want to cook. Her seascapes and scenery are moving and make you happy even if you cannot go there. I love Dave Brown's engaging design and the way he used the sea and landscape and enmeshed the beautiful photos from all over the Mediterranean, some of them his own, in a poetic net. Thank you, Susan and Dave, for turning the book into a work of art.

I have many thanks, too, for the Ebury team who worked on the production, sales, and marketing of *Mediterranean*: Lucy Harrison, Stephenie Naulls, Claire Scott, Antony De Rienzo, and Fiona Atkinson; and for Vanessa Forbes and Anjali Nathani for deftly handling the foreign editions, Anjali also for setting up the Frankfurt Book Fair meeting.

I have huge thanks for Ten Speed Press for the splendid new American edition, for Lorena Jones for taking on the book, and my editors Emma Rudolph and Doug Ogan for making the conversions and Americanization and everything else happen so perfectly. I love Emma Campion's beautiful warm evocative cover. I am grateful to production designers Mari Gill and Faith Hague, production and prepress color manager Jane Chinn, publicist David Hawk, and marketers Samantha Simon and Windy Dorresteyn. Thank you all. I am thrilled to be your author.

As I cooked through *Mediterranean*, I thought affectionately of people I got to know in different countries while researching their food, especially those who cooked for me, taught me, and showed me around. They allowed me into their lives and came into mine. I am still in touch with many – we call, visit, and stay. I am forever grateful to them for enriching my life with so much more than recipes.

Published in the United States by Ten Speed Press, an imprint of Random House, a division of Penguin Random House LLC, New York.
www.tenspeed.com

This edition published by arrangement with Ebury Press. First published in the United Kingdom by Ebury Press, part of the Penguin Random House group of companies.

Library of Congress Control Number: 2021939414

Hardcover ISBN: 978-1-9848-5974-7
eBook ISBN: 978-1-9848-5975-4

Printed in China

Acquiring editor: Lorena Jones | Project editor: Emma Rudolph | Production editor: Doug Ogan
Designer: Dave Brown | Cover designer: Emma Campion
Production designers: Mari Gill and Faith Hague | Production manager: Jane Chinn
Recipe tester: Sandy Gluck | Food and prop stylist: Frankie Unsworth
Americanizer: Kate Slate | Proofreader: Rachel Markowitz | Indexer: Ken DellaPenta
Publicist: David Hawk | Marketers: Samantha Simon and Windy Dorresteyn

10 9 8 7 6 5 4 3 2

First US Edition